THE
SUPREME COURT
CHALLENGE AGAINST BILL-96 AND
QUEBEC'S SEPARATIST AGENDA
The Leave to Appeal for Access to Justice
in Defence of Our Canadian Identity

PETER TREMBLAY, ED.

THE INDEPENDENT
CANADIAN COMMISSION
ON HUMAN &
CIVIL RIGHTS

Agora Books

The Independent Canadian Commission on Human Rights
and The Agora Cosmopolitan

THE SUPREME COURT CHALLENGE AGAINST BILL-96 AND QUEBEC'S SEPARATIST AGENDA: The Leave to Appeal for Access to Justice in Defence of Our Canadian Identity

Agora Books
P.O. Box 24191
300 Eagleson Road
Kanata, Ontario K2M 2C3   CANADA

Agora Books is a self-publishing agency for authors that was launched by The Agora Cosmopolitan which is a registered not-for-profit corporation.

ISBN 978-1-77838-043-3

Printed in Canada

CONTENTS

Preface

THIS BOOK DOCUMENTS A LEAVE to Appeal in the Supreme Court of Canada that seeks to challenge the affirmation of the Government of Quebec's denial of access to justice to non-francophones through Bill-96. This new law is based upon an entirely artificial legal construction of a "Quebec nation," which not only violates fundamental human rights and the ideals of Western democracy but also perpetuates a corrupted version of the vital notion of the Canadian identity of francophones. This deception is the work of Archons in Quebec who seek to manipulate modern Quebec, shaping it into a reflection of the repressive mind of these elites.

The prevailing denial of access to justice in the Quebec court system to non-francophones, whose rights to free access to court interpreters were affirmed by previous decisions of the Supreme Court outlined in the Leave to Appeal, underscores the anti-human rights agenda of Bill-96 specifically, and the sovereignty efforts of the Quebec Establishment.

This agenda explains Premier Legault's decision to block access to Quebec emergency rooms for people who did not choose to take COVID-19 vaccines. The decision ignored the long list of well-documented side effects caused by these "vaccines," including numerous premature deaths. At the same time, the policy underscored a lack of consideration of basic human rights.

Another poignant demonstration of the Quebec government's hypocrisy on human rights has emerged more recently, forming the basis of the current Leave to Appeal. Judge Catherine Pilon of the Quebec Human Rights Tribunal denied fundamental access to justice on a claim approved by the Quebec Human Rights Commission. This began a path to the Supreme Court of Canada on behalf of the rights of all Canadians.

Before Catherine Pilon became a judge, she worked as a lawyer and senior partner at Dentons law firm for Quebec elites who sought to quash human rights claims. After she became a judge for the Quebec Court of Appeal and later the Quebec Human Rights Tribunal, it's apparent that the "leopard didn't change her spots," given her use of the judicial office to attack the fundamental rights of visible minorities and language minorities. In at least one photo online, she openly consorts with Quebec's political and other elites, representing a conflict with her judicial duties.

How can any government that professes a commitment to human rights appoint a judge who was a senior partner at an international law firm that multinational corporations have relied upon to subvert human rights claims to preside over a Human Rights Tribunal?

Francophones were the very first group to popularly refer to themselves as *Les Canadiens*. Canada has existed as an identifiable geographic space since 1535, long before there was a province of Quebec with the demarcation of the supposed "Quebec nation." Quebec is not a "distinct society." Rather, it is a province made up of many "distinct societies," which is the hallmark of any pluralistic society that is home to many communities that all deserve to be recognized and valued in a democracy.

What about Mohawk and other indigenous communities who speak languages other than French and whose ancestors were in the province of Quebec far longer than European and other settlers?

The Archons who control Quebec are no friends of the overwhelming majority of francophones and their non-francophone neighbours who all get along with each other. Such is the very spirit of the francophones who referred to themselves as "les habitants" and regarded themselves to be *Les Canadiens* long before any pretension of a "Quebec nation."

The Archons who control Quebec are essentially relics of the elites who ruled over New France as an extension of the authoritarian monarchy that ruled over France before the French Revolution. The *fleur-de-lys* was the emblem of the aristocracy of New France, which these elites sought to imprint onto Quebec's popular culture in the effort to concoct a revisionist "nation" to conceal the true identity of francophones in Quebec as *Canadiens*.

Relics like Premier Legault and the elites who form Quebec's new aristocracy reject the values of individualism, freedom, logic, and rights that were championed by the European Enlightenment. Premier Legault and his confederates view the state as the embodiment of the masses who should blindly follow their leaders. For them, the pursuit of rights, freedom, and logic leads to chaos; their creation of myths and "noble lies" are necessary for "public order."

The place of the *fleur-de-lys* and the idea of "nationhood" in Quebec are part of just such a system of "noble lies" that now manifests as the denial of access to justice in Quebec, along with other vital services to non-francophones, which goes against the values of the majority of francophones whose ancestors viewed their nation to be Canada.

The maple leaf was adopted as the first emblem to express French Canadian cultural survival, and not the *fleur-de-lys*, which was the adopted symbol of the French monarchy that French Canadians regarded as having abandoned them to the devices of the British.

This same group of francophones settled into a territory they called Canada and spread into all provinces and territories alongside Indigenous allies, the British, and other migrant populations. The Maple Leaf was adopted as Canada's symbol, inspired by the determination of French cultural survival.

A Department of Canadian Heritage document recalls that in 1834, the Société Saint-Jean-Baptiste, an association celebrating French-Canadian language and culture, adopted the maple leaf as an emblem.

The French-speaking newspaper *Le Canadien* adds a wreath of maple leaves to its front page, elaborating that as of 1836, "the maple leaf has been [...] adopted as the emblem of Lower Canada."

The relics of New France's aristocracy reject our Canadian maple leaf as the true symbol of French-Canadian cultural survival, opting instead for the *fleur-de-lys*. The separatists who preside over the Parti Quebecois and Quebec Solidaire on the provincial level, the Bloc Quebecois on the federal level, and the "pseudo-separatists" of Premier Legault's "CAQ" pursue treason against the *Canadiens* who envisioned a Canada from sea to sea to sea.

When the French Revolution came, the relics of colonial authority in New France were determined to preserve their power by asserting the need to defend the French language. But their real concern was to hang onto power as bloodline descendants of the former colonial rulers of New France. As these elite bloodlines worked to consolidate their authority in Lower Canada (1791-1840) after "The British Conquest" and into the Confederation of Canada after 1867, they eventually started to invent stories that Canada was the political creation of "Anglos" in Britain. These elites further proselytized through their political and other operatives that francophones should "follow their lead" if they wanted to preserve their "culture and identity" as Quebecois against Canada as the supposed enemy of French cultural survival.

In the 1950s, Quebec Premier Maurice Duplessis set the tone of an isolationist nationalism that sought to negotiate as much power as possible for the Province of Quebec against "Canada as an enemy," all in the name of protecting the French identity and language.

The true agenda of successive Quebec provincial governments into the current Premier François Legault government has always been to pursue self-aggrandizement for the rich and the powerful of Quebec through lies about Canada's true relationship to francophones. Disingenuous representations of this relationship are used to create mass hysteria among francophones in the province of Quebec about their imminent demise.

By painting such a grim picture of imminent demise, Legault seeks to manipulate francophones into believing that denying fundamental access to justice and other services to other language communities is necessary.

If Premier Legault's true agenda were to promote the French language, he would do that by promoting French-speaking Quebecois of diverse racial backgrounds, ethnicities, creeds, and social statutes, including people from Indigenous communities into senior positions of the Quebec government bureaucracy, the judiciary, police services, and elsewhere. This would inspire all these different communities to regard learning French as a means of getting access to new economic opportunities. Premier Legault would also be seeking to support a climate of economic investment and job creation for francophones along with other communities.

But all of this potential is subverted by oppressive legislation. These include language laws that consolidate control in the hands of the relics who preside over Quebec's largest corporations, oppressing not only non-francophones but many francophones as well, such as writers who have been forced to move out of Quebec and "anglicize" because of centralized legislative control of Quebec's book publishing industry. This policy prevents self-published francophone authors from being able to thrive as independent writers. This stands in stark contrast to English-speaking counterparts outside Quebec who can self-publish and have access to book retailers without the corporate control that exists in Quebec. These Quebec corporate publishing companies also serve the relics of the Quebec government by making sure that francophones in Quebec only get exposed to a propagandistic official narrative regarding Quebec as a "nation."

There are many immigrants who have learned French without the need for Bill-96. But Legault doesn't want to focus on them because that would conflict with his narrative "of all these damn immigrants only wanting to speak in English" which threatens the French language.

Apparently, Legault doesn't like to promote the success of immigrants who already speak French fluently, among other languages that they speak, because they pose a different threat that would not be politically correct for him to talk about. That threat for him seems to be the transformation of Quebec into a cosmopolitan society that speaks French but rejects the authority of the relics. It's simply easier for him to whip up mass hysteria about immigrants who "don't want to speak French" than to reveal the racist undertones of Quebec's nationalist agenda.

Quebec's relics don't want people whose names might sound like Friedman, Singh, Chang, Mohammed, Fernandez, Rossi, Yellow Feather, or any other such "non-New France" names rising to power and eventually becoming Premier, no matter how good their French is. This is evident in the absence of such people in positions of authority and explains why Legault apparently referred to Dominque Anglade, the leader of the Quebec Liberal Party and a visible minority, as "that lady."

The truth of the matter is that Quebec today is a province created through British colonial authority that contains a francophone population genetically related to the francophone population that migrated across Canada. These migrants across Canada continue to live as francophone communities whose constitutional rights have been recognized in the other provinces. These are rights that Quebec seeks to deny to anglophones in Quebec with particular reference to access to justice in the court system, which is fundamental to the affirmation of human and civil rights.

Discriminatory laws in Quebec like Bill-96 subvert the perception of Quebec as a progressive environment for investment and economic upward social mobility for everyone in Quebec. Such discriminatory laws also fundamentally subvert the rights and freedoms of Canadians in Quebec in ways that have nothing to do with protecting French.

Promoting French language and culture has not been a part of Legault's priorities because his rhetoric on the protection of the French language is simply propaganda.

Bill-96 and other such language policies show no gratitude to the Indigenous people who welcomed early settlers from different parts of France and the many different language communities who built Quebec and today support a rich diversity that francophones enjoy.

Bill-96 and other such language laws also show no gratitude to the many language communities across that provide Quebec with billions of dollars in transfer payments yearly.

The francophones who view cultural diversity as enriching their lives, who regard Bill-96 as incompatible with a just society where everyone thrives, express a modern vision of a longstanding Canadian francophone identity. This is the sense of French-Canadian identity that Legault rejects. Legault seeks to instill fear to support his efforts through Bill-96 to consolidate power for his quasi-separatist goals for Quebec.

Perhaps no modern francophone leader understood the hypocrisy of the relics who preside over Quebec than former Prime Minister Pierre Elliot Trudeau, who fought against the Quebec government's aims to recognize Quebec as a "distinct society" in the *Canadian Charter of Rights and Freedoms*. He appreciated that the aim of "distinct society" was not to protect the French language, but instead to legally justify the pursuit of the separation of Quebec from the rest of Canada without having to ever call another Referendum vote. His prime minister son, Justin Trudeau, appears to have sold out his father's legacy as a champion for Canadian national unity through his apparent silence on Bill-96, which suggests that he agrees with the separatist intentions of Bill-96 along with other grabs for power by the relics.

The Supreme Court of Canada challenge that is contained in this book provides insight into the nefarious agenda of proponents for a "Quebec nation" as expressed through the intentions of laws like Bill-96. This law seeks to declare French to be the "common language" of Quebec, which itself is an Algonquin word for "narrow passage" or "strait." Indeed Bill-96 denies Indigenous ancestral ties that are in the DNA of the overwhelming majority of francophones in Quebec whose ancestors referred to themselves as *Canadiens*.

PETER TREMBLAY

By concocting the notion of a "Quebec nation," elites seek to emphasize the imagery of the "ideal Quebecois" as descendants of white French-speaking settlers with no ties to Indigenous or other cultural affinities. This is evident in the images of the people in power of modern Quebec, who have decision-making authority in the police, the judiciary, public services, and corporations including media organizations. Quebec has a particularly glaring lack of cultural and ethnic diversity in these corridors of power. We can see Canada's varied ethnic and religious communities—such as Chinese, Indian, black, Jewish, Sikh, and Indigenous—in advertising and as spokespersons of government agencies and private corporations far more frequently outside of Quebec.

The Leave of Appeal contained herein shows how English-speaking people in Quebec are not entitled to the same rights as French-speaking people in Ontario and other parts of Canada. Regarding the justice system, the Leave to Appeal addresses efforts by Quebec to exclude itself from human rights obligations by enacting the "Notwithstanding Clause," which is Section 33 of *the Canadian Charter of Rights and Freedoms.*

The court challenge contained in this book seeks to pursue a National Constitutional Question regarding Bill-96 and other such legislation designed to attack civil and human rights.

This Constitutional Question aims to ask the Supreme Court of Canada to rule that the "Notwithstanding Clause," which enables governments to exclude their legislation from human rights constitutional protections, is an unconstitutional way to enable Bill-96 and other such laws.

Some key constitutional-related questions raised through this Supreme Court challenge:

Shouldn't any use of the "Notwithstanding Clause" that seeks to undermine Canada as a multicultural and bilingual society consisting of English-speaking and French-speaking Official Language communities as recognized by provisions of the Canadian Charter of Rights and Freedoms and accompanying human rights be declared unconstitutional?

Should francophone public entities like the Gatineau Police Service feel confident that they can trample the rights of non-francophones who don't have the money to hire an expensive francophone lawyer, simply by electing to speak French in court hearings?

Should the Government of Quebec be allowed to ignore the rule of law as it pertains to Supreme Court of Canada decisions that seek to affirm the Charter?

Should the minority rights of hundreds of thousands of Canadians in Quebec continue to be marginalized by francophone organizations that run roughshod over the rights of these minorities, backed by provincial government policies that ignore our fundamental rights and freedoms?

Carby-Samuels v. Ville de Gatineau is a Leave to Appeal application that affects the rights of hundreds of thousands of non-francophone Canadians within and outside the Province of Quebec who may need to pursue the affirmation of their civil and human rights in a Quebec courtroom.

A principal aim of the Leave to Appeal contained herein seeks to ask that the Supreme Court to declare illegal any use of the "Notwithstanding Clause" to deny fundamental human rights through Bill-96 and similar government bills.

By declaring the "Notwithstanding Clause" unconstitutional, we can begin to empower our court system to enforce national standards of civil and human rights against any and all efforts of governments in Canada to subvert them.

INTRODUCTION

The Supreme Court of Canada Challenge Against Quebec's Denial of Rights to Non-Francophones

T HE SUPREME COURT OF CANADA is currently reviewing a Leave to Appeal application against Ville de Gatineau. The case provides an indirect but significant challenge to the efforts of Premier François Legault and the province of Quebec to promote French as the "common language" in Quebec through Bill-96.

Raymond Carby-Samuels, who filed the Leave to Appeal application, is hoping to set a legal precedent for communities in Quebec that seek to push back against the quasi-separatist nationalistic government that wants to promote the French language at the cost of denying the rights of non-francophones.

Language minorities in and outside Quebec now exist in a state of imbalance. If Canada is to be a "united nation," it must recognize a set of fundamental rights and freedoms for everyone. Quebec's exclusionary language laws are at risk of undermining these Canadian values.

Indeed, our *Canadian Charter of Rights and Freedoms* is meaningless if large communities of people cannot defend their rights and freedoms in a court of law, simply because they cannot speak the language of court proceedings.

Furthermore, the idea that Canada is a country united by a set of democratic values lacks integrity if Quebec can simply ignore fundamental Charter rights and freedoms.

Outside of Quebec, francophones and members of other minority language communities are entitled to free access to an interpreter in all court hearings. The Supreme Court of Canada has made this clear. Yet, Quebec continues to deny similar rights to its very large English-speaking communities and "allophones," a uniquely Canadian term for speakers of languages other than English or French. Quebec's policies have empowered fully bilingual lawyers in Quebec to win their cases by default, simply by speaking French to prevent non-francophones from being able to defend against infringements of their rights.

A Government of Ontario website stipulates that the province provides more than 150,000 hours of free court interpreter services as a result of the Supreme Court of Canada's decisions; these are the same decisions that Quebec and its court system scandalously choose to ignore. Consideration is given to French speakers outside of Quebec, yet the province, which relies on substantive transfer payments from the other provinces, fails to offer the same courtesy to Quebec's non-Francophone population.

A new not-for-profit organization is seeking to challenge this national imbalance regarding basic access to justice. The Independent Canadian Commission on Civil and Human Rights, through the Leave to Appeal application of *Carby-Samuels v. Ville de Gatineau*, seeks to defend the rights of all Canadians to have free access to a court interpreter.

In this particular case, the Quebec Human Rights Commission originally sided in favour of Carby-Samuels, who experienced profound discrimination at the hands of the Gatineau Police Services.

During a Quebec Human Rights Tribunal held on May 24, 2023, DHC Avocats, the law firm representing the City of Gatineau, and Catherine Pilon, the presiding judge, began to engage in verbal exchanges about Carby-Samuels in French and refused to translate what they said into English. When these exchanges were later translated into English from a transcription of the proceeding, it was apparent that Carby-Samuels would have sought to object to the nature of these verbal exchanges. Yet, not a French speaker, he was unaware of what was said at the time, and the judge and lawyers refused to translate. This is despite the fact that this same lawyer had spoken entirely in English in the initial Quebec Human Rights Tribunal hearing in late December 2022.

Carby-Samuels sought to transfer his file to the Quebec Superior Court to seek judicial relief from the indignity he had experienced. But, at the Superior Court level, Carby-Samuels was again denied access to a free court interpreter.

Case management of the Quebec Court of Appeal informed Carby-Samuels that they would also not provide free access to a court interpreter. These events have precipitated the current Leave to Appeal application by Carby-Samuels.

In the name of "preserving the French language," the Government of Quebec, through Bill-96, has entirely destroyed the integrity of the *Canadian Charter of Rights and Freedoms* and, indeed, our very values as a pluralistic democracy.

The National Assembly in Quebec authorizes the Tribunal in Quebec to judicially review human rights cases. This same tribunal denies access to justice to non-francophones who are pitted against high-priced francophone lawyers whose clients have been assessed by the Quebec Human Rights Commission to have perpetrated infringements against the human rights code.

In a pluralistic democracy, the rights of everyone must be protected. Fundamentally, that must include access to justice through a court interpreter.

The Supreme Court of Canada has affirmed that the right to the assistance of an interpreter is a fundamental right grounded in the rules of natural justice (Tran, supra, page 963; *MacDonald v. City of Montreal*, [1986] 1 S.C.R. 460 at page 499; *Société des Acadiens v. Association of Parents*, [1986] 1 S.C.R. 549 at page 621, per Wilson J., concurring).

The Independent Canadian Commission of Civil and Human Rights believes that the French language can best be promoted by providing financial and other resources to educational, cultural, and literary activities that promote the French language.

Yet, Bill-96, along with Quebec's continued denial of free access to a court interpreter, is instead based upon a discriminatory premise that one group, which in this case are "French-Quebecois," have an inherently superior status that entitles this group to oppress or ignore the rights of others, including access to justice.

Efforts to extinguish the rights of others, including the denial of access to justice, are predicated on the use of force through oppressive laws and draconian policies. This is a foolish way to seek to protect the French language, especially given the French people's historical affinity with the cause of resisting inequality and social injustice. Average Quebecers of all languages seek to be good neighbours to each other. They share a set of common values that supports the pursuit of a just society for all. The denial of court interpreter services to non-francophones neither respects the values of average Quebecers nor the rule of law.

Carby-Samuels v. Ville de Gatineau is a Leave to Appeal application that affects the rights of hundreds of thousands of non-francophone Canadians within and outside the Province of Quebec who may need to pursue the affirmation of their civil and human rights in a Quebec courtroom.

Should francophone public entities like the Gatineau Police Service feel confident that they can trample the rights of non-francophones who don't have the money to hire an expensive francophone lawyer, simply by electing to speak French in court hearings?

Should the Government of Quebec be allowed to ignore the rule of law as it pertains to Supreme Court of Canada decisions that seek to affirm the Charter?

Should the minority rights of hundreds of thousands of Canadians in Quebec continue to be marginalized by francophone organizations that run roughshod over the rights of these minorities, backed by provincial government policies that ignore our fundamental rights and freedoms?

The Independent Canadian Commission on Civil and Human Rights invites interested parties to contact them through their HumanRightsCommission.ca website to get involved as interveners in a collective effort to reaffirm rights and freedoms in Quebec. The Commission seeks to promote French language and culture without subverting the integrity of the progressive values of our Charter.

Supreme Court of Canada Leave to Appeal

Raymond Carby-Samuels v. Ville de Gatineau et al.

File No._____

IN THE SUPREME COURT OF CANADA

(ON APPEAL FROM AN INTERIM JUDGEMENT OF QUEBEC HUMAN RIGHTS
TRIBUNAL AND THE SUPERIOR COURT OF QUEBEC)

BETWEEN:

RAYMOND CARBY-SAMUELS

APPLICANT (Appellant)

AND:

VILLE DE GATINEAU et al.

RESPONDENT (Respondent)

APPLICATION FOR LEAVE TO APPEAL

(Pursuant to s. 40 of the Supreme Court of Canada Act and Rule 25(1), 43.1

Of the Rules of the Supreme Court of Canada)

Raymond Carby-Samuels

Self-Represented Litigant.

Member, Canadian Bar Association

Tel: (514) 712-7516

Email: cosmopolita_rc@yahoo.com,

lawsociety.carby.samuels@utoronto.ca

Suite 325 - 207 Bank Street

Ottawa, Ontario   K2P 2N2

DHC AVOCATS

Counsel for the Respondent

Suite 4500

800, Square Victoria

Montreal, Quebec H4Z 1J2

E-mail: mdaponte@dhcavocats.ca

TABLE OF CONTENTS

File No._____

IN THE SUPREME COURT OF CANADA

(ON APPEAL FROM AN INTERIM JUDGEMENT OF THE QUEBEC HUMAN RIGHTS TRIBUNAL AND THE SUPERIOR COURT OF QUEBEC)

BETWEEN:

RAYMOND CARBY-SAMUELS

APPLICANT (Appellant)

AND:

VILLE DE GATINEAU et al.

RESPONDENT (Respondent)

NOTICE OF APPLICATION FOR LEAVE TO APPEAL

(Pursuant to s. 40 of the *Supreme Court of Canada Act* and Rule 25(1), 43.1

Of the *Rules of the Supreme Court of Canada*)

TAKE NOTICE that Raymond Carby-Samuels (the **"Applicant"**) applies for leave to

appeal to the Court, under s. 40 of the Supreme Court Act and rule 25(1) of the Rules

of the Supreme Court of Canada, from the judgement of the Quebec Human Rights Tribunal,

File No: 550-53-000051-220 and the Quebec Superior Court, File No. 550-17-012903-231 made

on May 24, 2023, and for an order:

1.   granting leave to appeal;

2.   if leave to appeal is granted, ordering costs to the Applicant; and

3.   any further or other order that the court may deem appropriate.

AND FURTHER, TAKE NOTICE that this application for leave is made on the following grounds:

1. The ability of litigants to understand the language being used in the courtroom is fundamental to the ability of litigants to defend their rights as affirmed in law;

2. It is impossible for anyone to defend their rights in the courtroom if they don't understand the language being used in the courtroom;

3. Efforts that seek to protect the rights of one official language community cannot be held as legitimate if those efforts subvert the ability of individuals from another official language community to apply to a court of competent jurisdiction as guaranteed by Section 24(1) of the *Canadian Charter of Rights and Freedoms* in order to avail themselves of their rights in the officially bilingual society that Canada represents;

4. Quebec courts and tribunals are denying access to free court interpretation services to English-speaking people who cannot afford private language interpreter services for court hearings involving francophone litigants who choose only to address the Court, including litigants, in French. Translation services are essential for English speakers (and other members of language minorities) who seek to participate in court and tribunal hearings in the province of Quebec. Such free court interpreter services are available to French-speaking people outside of the province of Quebec, so the absence of English translation in Quebec courts violates principles of equity fundamental to the legal construction of Canada as an officially bilingual country.

5. The failure of Quebec courts to accommodate anglophones and other language minorities in Quebec is unconstitutional because such a failure ignores provisions of the *Canadian*

Charter of Rights and Freedoms, further reinforced by Supreme Court of Canada decisions that recognize access to such interpreter services as a "natural right."

6. If Quebec chooses to remain in Canada, which defines itself as a bilingual country, then its laws must respect the basic legal axiom that English-speaking individuals in Quebec ought to expect equivalent access to court interpreter services as French-speaking individuals outside of Quebec as *per* the outcome of Supreme Court of Canada rulings regarding the rights of members of Official Language communities across Canada.

AND FURTHER, TAKE NOTICE that the following documents will be referred to in support of this application for leave:

i.   E-mailed direction from the Quebec Court of Appeal;

ii.   Reasons for interim judgement rendered by the Quebec Superior Court;

iii. Transcript of Quebec Superior Court Trial dated May 24, 2023;

iv.   Reasons for interim judgement rendered by the Quebec Human Rights Tribunal;

v.   Transcript of the Quebec Human Rights Tribunal dated March 15, 2023;

vi.   Ontario court confirmation of free court interpreter services to francophones;

And other such further material that may be required and permitted.

AND FURTHER, TAKE NOTICE that this application for leave is made on the following grounds:

1.   The Quebec Human Rights Tribunal and subsequently the Quebec Superior Court (and the Quebec Court of Appeal via emailed corroboration) erred in law by deeming that neither the Canadian constitution in general nor preceding decisions of the Supreme Court in Canada, specifically, make it necessary for all criminal court, civil court, and administrative tribunals in Quebec to provide English-speaking litigants in Quebec (as part of an Official Languages minority) with free access to court interpreter services, bearing in mind that such a law has motivated courts outside of Quebec in Canada to provide such services to French-speaking minorities.

Dated at Ottawa, Ontario this 14th day of July, 2023.

SIGNED BY:

_____

Raymond Carby-Samuels

Self-Represented Litigant & Member, Canadian Bar Association

Suite 325, 207 Bank Street

Ottawa, Ontario K2P 2N2

Tel: (514) 712-7516

E-mails: lawsociety.carby.samuels@utoronto.ca, cosmopolita_rc@yahoo.com

5

ORIGINAL TO: THE REGISTRAR

COPY TO:

DHC AVOCATS

Suite 4500

800, Square Victoria

Montreal, Quebec H4Z 1J2

Me Mathieu Daponte

Tel: (514) 392-5709

Fax: (514) 331-0514

mdaponte@dhcavocats.ca

Counsel of the Respondents

NOTICE TO THE RESPONDENT OR INTERVENER: A respondent or intervener may serve and file a memorandum in response to this application for leave to appeal within 30 days of the date a file number is assigned in this matter. You will receive a copy of the letter to the applicant confirming the file number as soon as it is assigned. If no response is filed within that time, the Registrar will submit this application for leave to appeal to the Court for consideration

Ray S <raycosmopolite@gmail.com>

Jun 18,
2023,
7:23 PM

Does the Quebec Court of Appeal provide free court interpreter services for anlgophones during   court hearings and other proceedings if the opposing lawyer chooses to address the court in French?

Thanks for your consideration,

Raymond Samuels

C

Cour d'appel Montréal

Jun 19,
2023,
11:25 A
M

Hi,

-        **In criminal matters**: Interpretation services are provided to parties who do not understand the language used at the hearing. The costs are borne by the Ministère de la Justice.
-        **In civil matters**: Parties who do not understand the language used at the hearing must retain the services of an interpreter and pay the costs themselves.

Best regards,

Cour d'appel du Québec
Édifice Ernest Cormier
100, rue Notre-Dame Est
Montréal (Québec) H2Y 4B6

Téléphone : 514.393.2022
Télécopieur : 514.864.7270

SUPERIOR COURT

CANADA
PROVINCE OF QUEBEC
DISTRICT OF GATINEAU

No.:   550-17-012903-231

DATE: May 24, 2023

_____

BY THE HONOURABLE   CAROLE THERRIEN J.S.C. (JT 1581)

_____

RAYMOND SAMUELS
      Plaintiff
v.

VILLE DE GATINEAU ET ALS
      Defendants

_____

INCIDENTIAL JUDGMENT
ON ORAL OBJECTION OF THE PLAINTIFF[1]

_____

OVERVIEW

[1] Mr. Samuels introduced a proceeding before the Human Rights Tribunal against the City of Gatineau and police officers employed by the municipality. In that context, an interlocutory decision was rendered, which he believes is prejudicial to his fundamental rights.

[2] Therefore, he introduced the present proceedings before the Superior Court: *Application for leave to appeal a judgment rendered in the course of the preceding.*

_____

[1] Ce jugement peut être traduit en anglais à la demande de l'une ou l'autre des parties. Les instructions et le formulaire appropriés sont joints. This judgment may be translated into English at the request of either party. The appropriate instructions and form are attached.

[3] The defendants consider that the Court of Appeal is appointed by law to hear an appeal in the present case, and that interlocutory judgments are not appealable. Therefore, they introduced a motion asking the Court to (1) decline jurisdiction and (2) dismiss the applicant's motion.

[4] In the context of the hearing of that motion, the applicant raised a preliminary objection stating that he has the right to have the defendant's proceedings translated into English and have a free translator provided for him to be able to understand the attorney's oral arguments.

[5] The present judgment is only deciding on that objection.

ANALYSIS

[6] The plaintiff submits that he can't understand French and can't afford a translator. The proceeding is written in French and the attorney addresses the Court in French. The applicant can submit his arguments and proceedings in English.

[7] He was offered the opportunity revise his decision to represent himself and hire a translator. He declined.

[8] The present case is a civil matter. The Court spoke to the applicant in English. At any point, the applicant would have to speak French. The defendants don't ask him or the Court to force him to write or speak French. The issue is only about forcing the attorney to speak and write in English, or for the Court to provide, free of charge, a translator to the applicant.

[9] The applicant states that the situation violates his constitutional rights, section 14 of the Canadian charter of rights and 36 of the Charter of rights and freedom which read as follows:

> **14** A party or witness in any proceedings who does not understand or speak the language in which the proceedings are conducted or who is deaf has the right to the assistance of an interpreter.[2]

> **36.** Every accused person has a right to be assisted free of charge by an interpreter if he does not understand the language used at the hearing or if he is deaf.[3]

[10]   The civil code of procedures provides that:

---

[1] The Constitution Act, 1982, Schedule B to the Canada Act 1982 (UK). 1982, c 11,

[3] Charter of human rights and freedoms, Chapter C-12;

550-17-012903-231

INTERPRETATION SERVICES

298. To facilitate the examination of a witness, the court may retain the services of an interpreter.

The interpreter's remuneration is borne by the Minister of Justice if one of the parties is a beneficiary, in the judicial districts of Abitibi and Roberval, under the agreement approved by the Act approving the Agreement concerning James Bay and Northern Québec (chapter C-67) or, in the judicial district of Mingan, under the agreement approved by the Act approving the Northeastern Québec Agreement (chapter C-67.1).

299. A witness who is unable to hear or to speak by reason of a disability may take the oath and testify by any means enabling them to express themselves. If such means are unavailable, the witness may be assisted by an interpreter, whose remuneration is borne by the Minister of Justice.

[11] And finally, the Constitution also provides that:

19 (1) Either English or French may be used by any person in, or in any pleading in or process issuing from, any court established by Parliament.

[12] The defendants submit that the Supreme Court has confirmed their right to write and speak French in the present proceeding.[4]

[13] The law is clear. The Court has no discretion, in the present civil matter in the district of Gatineau, to order the Minister of Justice to provide and pay for translation of the arguments and written proceedings of the defendants, for the applicant's benefit.

[14] The Court reiterates the possibility for the applicant to hire such a translator, an option that was not satisfactory for the applicant.

[15] In the present situation, where the applicant is not an *accused*, the right to an interpreter does not imply the right to a free translation, nor an obligation for the other parties to speak his language. Moreover, his right to speak and plea in English is fully recognized and respected.

FOR THESE REASONS, THE COURT:

[16] **DISMISSES** the objection of the applicant;

[17] **SCHEDULES** the hearing of the defendants declinatory motion on June 5, 2023;

---

[4] Mazraani v. Industrial Alliance Insurance and Financial Services Inc., 2018 3 SCR 261;

550-17-012903-231

[18]   Costs, to follow the final decision.

_____
CAROLE THERRIEN, J.C.S.

The applicant is self represented

Me Mathieu Daponte
Defendant's attorney

Hearing date: May 23, 2023

HIS MAJESTY THE KING
_____

CANADA

PROVINCE OF QUEBEC

Case No. 550-17-012903-231

_____

P R O C E E D I N G S

BEFORE THE HONOURABLE JUDGE CAROLE THERRIEN

MAY 24, 2023

_____

APPEARANCES:

Mr. M. Daponte   For the Defendant

Briaris Transcription Services

TABLE OF CONTENTS

DATE TRANSCRIPT COMPLETED: June 14, 2023

DATE TRANSCRIPT ORDERED: June 17, 2023

Briaris Transcription Services

1

2   PROCEEDING COMMENCED...

3

4   JUDGE THERRIEN: Mr. Samuels, this morning, we're

5   here to decide on... well, not necessar- I will not decide

6   this morning, I can tell you that first -- the first thing.

7   I will -- I will hear your arguments and hear the -- the

8   city's arguments, and I will decide later on a written

9   document. So I'm here to... So, the first thing is that I

10   will hear your arguments against the motion, and then...

11   well, first, I'll hear the arguments of the -- the -- the

12   city, and then yours, and deci- and -- and I will decide on a

13   -- a written decision. So are you still there, Mr. Samuels?

14   MR. SAMUELS: Yes, Your Honour.

15   JUDGE THERRIEN: Oh, okay.

16   MR. SAMUELS: Yes. This is Raymond Samuels again,

17   member of the Canadian Bar Association. May I make an

18   objection to start things off before we get into the

19   proceedings itself?

20   JUDGE THERRIEN: Well, usually, it's not the way to

21   do it, but wha- anyway, I -- I -- I will hear what you have

22   to say. And again, I can't see you. Are -- are you sure

23   that your camera is on?

24   MR. SAMUELS: I'm not sure, Your Honour. I'm not

25   sure.

1   JUDGE THERRIEN: Okay.

2   MR. SAMUELS: Does it need to be on or... I just

3 wanted to make sure.

4   JUDGE THERRIEN: Oh, okay.

5   MR. SAMUELS: Does it need to be on, Your Honour?

6   JUDGE THERRIEN: Now I can't see you. There -- the -

7 - on your screen, there's a -- there's a... how can I say

8 that? A bandeau on the top. There are --

9   MR. SAMUELS: Mh'mh.

10   JUDGE THERRIEN: -- little signs on the top.

11   MR. SAMUELS: Mh'mh.

12   JUDGE THERRIEN: And one -- one is a camera. It

13 looks like a camera. If you -- if you click on it, maybe...

14 No? Oh. Oh, oh. There's a movement. There. I can see you

15 now. Okay, good.

16   MR. SAMUELS: Okay.

17   JUDGE THERRIEN: Okay.

18   MR. SAMUELS: Okay, Your Honour. Yes, Your

19 Honour. So yes, so this is Raymond Samuels, member of the

20 Canadian Bar Association. I wanted to start things off by a-

21 objecting to the submission by the City of -- of Gatineau

22 based upon a Charter objection, section 14 of the Canadian

23 Charter of Rights and Freedoms. This particular

24 representation was sent to me by the City of Gatineau's

25 lawyer, Mathieu Turcotte, completely in French. I sent a

1 note to Mathieu Turcotte objecting, saying that it was

2 unilingual French. Mathieu Turcotte speaks English very

3 well. He refused to make any accommodation to get this

4 document in a -- in an English form. Based upon the -- the

5 documentation that this court already has, the Canadian --

6 the Supreme Court of Canada disclar- declared a mistrial over

7 the refusal to have documents translated based upon section

8 14 of the Canadian Charter of -- of Rights and Freedoms,

9 which deal with the right of an interpreter. The -- the

10 judge of the Supreme Court of Canada explicitly said, the ru-

11 the right of section 14 of the Charter is one held not only

12 by accused persons, but also by the parties in civil actions

13 and administrative proceedings and by witnesses. So in light

14 of the City of Gatineau's refute to -- to -- to, in my view,

15 exploit my -- my inability to understand the nature of their

16 representation to the court, I would lo- respectfully requ-

17 request, Your Honour, that their -- that their -- that their

18 legal eff- efforts today be rejected with costs based upon

19 the Ch- the Supreme Court of Canada ruling in terms of the

20 right of interpretation. In my view, they do not have a

21 right today to make representations to the court based upon

22 explicit and ongoing Charter violations. They sent me this

23 notice today completely in French. I objected. I sent a

24 representation to them, Your Honour. They didn't even have

25 the courtesy of answering, which is -- which -- and -- and I

1   -- I -- I -- which -- which are -- in my view, I'm

2   additionally shocked by. They failed to have any court- they

3   -- they -- I -- I sent them an email, they don't have -- they

4   don't even have the courtesy to respond. And in my view,

5   sending a legal notice along with representations comple- to

6   -- and in a language other than the litigant can understand

7   is not only against the Charter, but it's discourteous. And

8   in my view, based upon my efforts to try to resolve this

9   today by -- by -- by asking them to -- by -- by -- by re-

10 informing them that I can't understand what they're, you

11 know, the -- the nature of their representation today. I

12 would like this thrown out. Because I've -- because it's not

13 --

14   JUDGE THERRIEN: Okay.

15   MR. SAMUELS: -- because I've -- I've -- I've --

16 I've made multiple representations to them and they've

17 refused to accommodate. And now they're trying to exploit my

18 inability to understand their representation today. They're

19 trying to, you know, by, you know -- they're trying to

20 exploit my inability to understand French today, and it's a

21 violation of the Charter. So, in my view, they do not have a

22 -- they do not have a constitutional authority to be

23 presenting to the court today based upon explicit ru- rulings

24 by the Supreme Court of Canada on this matter, Your Honour.

25   JUDGE THERRIEN: Okay. So, Madame -- I -- I will

1 address the clerk at this point. Madame la Greffière, s'il

2 vous --

3   THE CLERK: Oui.

4   JUDGE THERRIEN: -- plaît noter -- et ce procès-

5 verbal, je vais vous demander de le rédiger en anglais, s'il

6 vous plaît.

7   THE CLERK: Okay.

8   JUDGE THERRIEN: Est-ce que vous êtes capables?

9   THE CLERK: Je vais -- je vais essayer. Et puis

10 je pourrais vous le -- le donner au [inaudible].

11   JUDGE THERRIEN: Très bien. So, "The court

12 acknowledges the preliminary objection of the applicant based

13 on section 14 of the Canadian Charter of Rights related to

14 the non-translation of the defendant's procedures. Motivated

15 by the impossibility of the defendant to understand the

16 defendant's arguments and his own impossibility to have

17 translation services." Maître Daponte, est-ce que je note

18 que vous ne vous exprimerez pas non plus en anglais?

19   MR. DAPONTE: Effectivement, Monsieur le Juge.

20   JUDGE THERRIEN: Ok. On va -- je vais l'ajouter, on

21 ne va pas s'en changer. Paragraphe.

22   "The court acknowledges that the defendant confirm that

23 neither the procedures nor the oral arguments will be

24 provided primarily in English nor translated by the

25 defendants." So, Mr. Samuels, I'll -- I will address Maître

1 Daponte. I have no possibility this morning to have any

2 translation provided and I will not decide on your motion

3 this morning. I will --

4   MR. SAMUELS: Okay. May I add too --

5   JUDGE THERRIEN: Let me finish, please.

6   MR. SAMUELS: Sorry, Your Honour. Sorry, Your

7 Honour.

8   JUDGE THERRIEN: I will render a written judgement on

9 that issue, and after that the -- I -- it -- it will be

10 decided on the -- the motion itself, okay? But this morning,

11 I will hear the city and the other defendants' arguments on

12 the issue of translation, on the issue that you are raising

13 this morning, okay? And after my judgement, that will not be

14 rendered today. It will be rendered on a written document

15 that will be in English for you -- I'm -- I'm just advising

16 you. I will render it in English, and you will be provided

17 with that judgement, and then the -- the -- the -- the

18 procedures will continue only after that. So, this morning,

19 I will not decide on the procedure that's being introduced by

20 the city. I will decide on your motion first, okay? So,

21 now, I will give the city the -- the possibility to address

22 the issue -- the issue that you are raising this morning. I

23 understand that you cannot understand the issues, that -- the

24 -- the -- sorry, the arguments, but I will summarise them

25 after, okay? So I will let Maître Daponte address the court.

Briaris Transcription Services

1   MR. DAPONTE: D'accord, Madame la Juge. Je

2   comprends l'orientation que souhaite prendre le tribunal. Je

3   -- j'attire respectueusement votre attention qu'il y a une

4   autre date de présentation qui a été instituée par Monsieur

5   le cinq juin. Donc, avec l'accord du tribunal, je demanderai

6   également que cette date soit repoussée après votre jugement

7   écrit concernant la question des droits linguistiques, si on

8   peut l'appeler ainsi.

9   JUDGE THERRIEN: Okay.

10   MR. DAPONTE: And --

11   JUDGE THERRIEN: Ju- just a second. I will just

12   translate that -- that --

13   MR. DAPONTE: Okay.

14   JUDGE THERRIEN: -- part to M. Samuels. So, Mr.

15   Samuels, Mr. -- Maître Daponte informs me at this point that

16   there's another date that you've -- you've asked for, which

17   is June 5th for -- I don't know which matter is was supposed

18   to be taken care of on -- at that day, but he's asking me

19   that this date will -- will be postponed until my judgement

20   on the -- let's say... the French-English issue is decided

21   by me. So this is -- it's -- I guess it's not an issue,

22   so... Maître Daponte, you may continue.

23   MR. DAPONTE: Merci. Bon... Madame la Juge, je

24   crois que c'est important de revenir sur le contexte qui a

25   amené Monsieur en cour supérieure aujourd'hui. En fait...

1   puis je -- je -- je vais mentionner sommairement les motifs

2   qui nous ont amenés à déposer une demande en irrecevabilité

3   mais aussi en -- en moyen déclinatoire de compétence par

4   rapport à la compétence de la cour supérieure. C'est-à-dire

5   que Monsieur, de ce que l'on comprend, souhaite appeler d'une

6   décision d'un jugement intérimaire au tribunal des droits de

7   la personne. Mais plutôt que de le faire à la cour d'appel,

8   comme l'enjoint l'article 132 de la Charte des droits et

9   libertés de la personne, Monsieur est plutôt devant la Cour

10 supérieure du Québec, alors que l'article 132 de la -- de la

11 Charte en question prévoit bien que les jugements finaux du

12 tribunal des droits de la personne peuvent, sous permission,

13 être appelés devant la cour --

14   JUDGE THERRIEN: Oui.

15   MR. DAPONTE: -- d'appel.

16   JUDGE THERRIEN: Oui.

17   MR. DAPONTE: J'at- -- je -- je précise parce que

18 justement le jugement interlocutoire dont il est question

19 aujourd'hui est celui de l'Honorable Juge Catherine Pilon, la

20 juge de la Cour du Québec, et dans le procès-verbal qui

21 correspond à la... audit jugement, qui est daté du 13 mai --

22 du 15 m- -- du 15 mars 2023, la Juge Pilon justement a

23 tranché la question dont il est question à nouveau

24 aujourd'hui, c'est-à-dire que Monsieur Samuels exigeait que

25 l'avocat qui représentait la ville de Gatineau parle anglais,

1 et il exigeait, de ce que l'on comprend, les services d'un

2 interprète. La juge lui rappelait à ce moment-là que c'était

3 de sa responsabilité d'en requérir les services. Donc je --

4 je voulais simplement le mentionner pour indiquer que la

5 question, à notre sens, a déjà fait l'objet d'une décision en

6 bonne et due forme.

7   JUDGE THERRIEN: Je comprends.

8   MR. DAPONTE: Monsieur souhaite se pourvoir en

9 appel de cette -- de ce jugement. Ce n'est pas encore le cas

10 aujourd'hui, mais on comprend que c'est son intention du

11 moins. À notre sens, donc, il n'y a pas eu lieu de refaire

12 le même débat aujourd'hui, il y a une certaine chose jugée à

13 cet égard-là. Puis quant au fond des choses, il nous semble

14 que la Cour supérieure n'est pas en compétence

15 respectueusement soumis d'entendre le présent litige, puisque

16 c'est de la juridiction de la cour d'appel d'entendre les

17 appels en provenance du tribunal des droits de la personne.

18   JUDGE THERRIEN: Bien.

19   MR. DAPONTE: Aussi... je vais aller sur le fond

20 des choses également, pas sur le fond des choses, mais par

21 rapport directement à l'argument de Monsieur si vous me le

22 permettez. On comprend effectivement que Monsieur souhaite

23 forcer une autre partie, le procureur d'une autre partie à

24 s'exprimer dans la langue officielle qui est la sienne,

25 l'anglais. Je comprends que Monsieur soulève un argument --

1   un jugement de la Cour supérieure qu'il n'a -- de la Cour

2   suprême, excusez-moi, qu'il n'a pas identifié, qui

3   concernerait précisément cette question-là. De notre côté,

4   je vous soumets une autre jurisprudence qui est tout à fait à

5   l'effet inverse, et ce en contexte d'une partie non

6   représentée. C'est l'affaire bien connue Mazraani

7   c. Industrielle Alliance, Assurance et services financiers in

8   c., à la référence 2018CSC50. Et puis je vous réfère tout

9   particulièrement aux paragraphes 34, 35, 36 et 39 du jugement

10   dans lequel la Cour suprême est très claire. Elle indique

11   que : "La présence d'une partie non représentée par avocat

12   n'entraîne pas la suspension des droits linguistiques

13   fondamentaux de quiconque", et plus particulièrement au

14   paragraphe 36, il est spécifié que : "La décision d'une

15   partie de ne pas se prévaloir de son droit à une interprète

16   ne doit jamais être utilisée pour contraindre les autres

17   parties, les témoins, les avocats, peu importe, à s'exprimer

18   dans la langue officielle de cette partie." Puis la Cour

19   suprême fait différents commentaires sur la façon dont --

20   dont il faut adresser cette situation lorsqu'elle se soulève

21   devant un tribunal. Puis la Cour suprême, au paragraphe 34

22   de cette décision -- de ce jugement, que je peux vous envoyer

23   si vous me le permettez --

24   JUDGE THERRIEN: Ça va aller.

25   MR. DAPONTE: -- indique que -- indique qu'une

1 telle demande est une violation de -- de l'article 133 de la

2 loi constitutionnelle --

3   MR. SAMUELS: Excuse me. How -- how am I supposed

4 to follow this when -- when it's all in French? I object to

5 this whole proceeding.

6   JUDGE THERRIEN: Okay. Okay.

7   MR. SAMUELS: It's -- it -- I -- I --

8   JUDGE THERRIEN: Mr. Samuels --

9   MR. SAMUELS: -- cannot follow argument in French.

10   JUDGE THERRIEN: -- Mr. Samuels, give me a second. I

11 will summarise it for you. Okay at this point?

12   MR. SAMUELS: Well, it can't -- it can't -- it

13 can't just be summarised, Your Honour. He's making very

14 nuanced arguments in French and I -- and I have to be able to

15 have the position to go to -- For you to make a decision,

16 Your Honour, I have to go through his line by line,

17 everything he says. It cannot be a summary. It has to be a

18 translation, it must be word for word and stuff for me to

19 make a credible representation to, you know, to him, to all

20 his legal arguments, and I can't do that if he's just going

21 on and on in French, you know? This is completely

22 unconstitutional. I'm not going to be able to provide

23 critical arguments to your Honour. If he is going on and on

24 in French, I cannot -- I -- I will not be able to, you know,

25 pro- provide a nuanced argument. So I completely object to

1   this whole proceeding. It's a violation of my rights. He's

2   -- the -- the -- this proceeding cannot continue in French

3   like this. It's a -- it's a complete violation of -- of my

4   rights to an interpreter. The interpretation must be word

5   for word. It can't be a summary. So I completely object to

6   the -- to -- to this proceeding. It is -- is -- it's

7   disenfranchising me. He's handicapping my ability to provide

8   you with a credible response, Your Honour. So I object to

9   him -- I object to this proceeding, and him going on in

10   French. Mr. Turcotte speaks English perfectly well. I don't

11   understand why they put -- why a Francophone is making

12   representations in a manner which I can't understand as -- as

13   an Anglophone. There's no way I'm going to be able to defend

14   myself in this proceeding if he's just going on and on in

15   French.

16   JUDGE THERRIEN: Okay.

17   MR. SAMUELS: So I object to this proceeding.

18   JUDGE THERRIEN: Okay. Madame la Greffière --

19   THE CLERK: Oui.

20   JUDGE THERRIEN: -- please note, "Mr. Samuels's

21   objection for the county --

22   MR. SAMUELS: The Supreme Court --

23   JUDGE THERRIEN: Let me --

24   MR. SAMUELS: -- in Canada say- --

25   JUDGE THERRIEN: Sir, if you --

Briaris Transcription Services

1	MR. SAMUELS:	Sorry, Your Honour.
2	JUDGE THERRIEN:	Let me --
3	MR. SAMUELS:	Sorry, Your Honour.
4	JUDGE THERRIEN:	-- do my job, please.
5	MR. SAMUELS:	Sorry, Your Honour.

6   JUDGE THERRIEN: So I'm just -- I'm just asking the

7   clerk to note what -- the following, okay? So, "The court

8   acknowledges Mr. Samuels's objection for the procedure to

9   continue without translation. The court rejects the

10   objection." Mr. Samuels, I will explain in my written

11   judgment the basics of my decision. Again, I'm -- I'm not

12   obligated to, but I will summarise the -- the... what --

13   what the -- the -- Maître Daponte just told me. So he

14   basically said that the objection you're ma- -- you're

15   submitting here, in this pre- the present -- the present

16   proceeding in front of the -- the Superior Court, is exactly

17   the same that you've submitted to the tribunal des droits de

18   la personne. And that he's... he's submitting that the

19   Supreme Court in 2018, in a decision named Mazraani c.

20   Industriel Alliance, said at paragraph 34 to 39 that the --

21   that -- that -- the -- the -- what happened -- what -- what's

22   happening here right now is not unconstitutional. So -- and

23   it's not a violation of your rights to have the -- the

24   opponents to express themselves in -- in French, without - in

25   civil cases I precise - without translation. And previous to

26

1   that argument, he submitted that -- he -- he referred to the

2   context of the present hearing, which originated -- which --

3   which -- which he submits that I don't have jurisdiction

4   considering that your -- you -- the question you're asking

5   the Superior Court should be addressed to the Court of

6   Appeals. Okay. So, did you -- did you -- At this point, I

7   will ask you a question, Mr. Samuels. Have you thought about

8   asking -- instead of being in the Superior Court, have you

9   thought about asking the Court of Appeals to quash the

10   decision that you are complaining about? And --

11   MR. SAMUELS: Okay. So, Your Honour -- so, Your

12   Honour, my objective -- and -- and again, the defendants will

13   be se- -- will be served today by a bailiff. I am getting --

14   I have applied to the court to get my -- to get the Quebec --

15   the current Quebec Human Rights Tribunal case transferred to

16   the Superior Court. I've sent an application to the Superior

17   Court about this, and the defendants are being served

18   documents regarding of this, in the particular matter. In

19   this particular matter, where the... where the defendants

20   cite. The defendants are citing, yes, in terms of the Court

21   of Appeals, if I was appealing a final decision of the court

22   of the -- of the Quebec Human Rights Tribunal, then the step,

23   the logical step in that particular situation would be to go

24   -- to go to the Court of Appeals. But this is not -- this is

25   not a -- a -- a step -- that type of situation. This is a

16

Briaris Transcription Services

1 situation whereby I am going to the Superior Court to get

2 their opinion on ex- on an explicit constitutional matters --

3   JUDGE THERRIEN: Okay.

4   MR. SAMUELS: -- that -- that I use -- that I --

5 that -- that -- that the Superior Court has jurisdiction of.

6   JUDGE THERRIEN: Okay.

7   MR. SAMUELS: And with that in mind, not only am I

8 seeking the opinion of the Superior Court, I'm getti- I'm

9 thinking for my whole entire case from the Tribunal to be

10 moved to the Superior Court based upon the points raised in

11 my appli- a leave of application to the -- to the Superior

12 Court.

13   JUDGE THERRIEN: Okay.

14   MR. SAMUELS: So I'm seeking for my whole case to

15 be transferred --

16   JUDGE THERRIEN: Okay.

17   MR. SAMUELS: -- Your Honour, --

18   JUDGE THERRIEN: Okay.

19   MR. SAMUELS: -- to the Superior Court.

20   JUDGE THERRIEN: Okay.

21   MR. SAMUELS: That's my objective.

22   JUDGE THERRIEN: Okay. Okay. So, I will let Maître

23 Daponte finish since I've decided that I will hear the -- the

24 -- the -- the matter if -- if -- because I need to render a

25 decision, and then it will be -- I will give you the

1 opportunity to complete your representations only on the

2 issue of the translation at this point. And like I said

3 earlier, I will not decide today. I will not render an oral

4 decision. I will render a written decision that you will

5 receive in a few days. So, Maître Daponte, si vous voulez

6 bien terminer. If you will please finish your arguments. We

7 were on the -- you were referring me to the Superior -- the

8 Supreme Court's decision rendered in 2018, Mazraani

9 c. Industrielle Alliance, paragraph 34 to 39. And your --

10 your point of view is -- to the effect that in -- in the

11 scope of that decision, the proceeding in the -- in the --

12 the present case is not against the -- the -- the Charter of

13 Rights, section 4- 14.

14   MR. DAPONTE: Exactement, Madame la Juge. Donc,

15 j'avais à peu près terminé.

16   JUDGE THERRIEN: Okay.

17   MR. DAPONTE: Je -- j'attire aussi l'attention du

18 tribunal puisque j'ai -- j'ai énoncé les différents

19 paragraphes auxquels je faisais référence, au paragraphe 35,

20 où il est indiqué que lorsqu'un tribunal constate que

21 justement qu'une partie plaidera dans une langue officielle

22 qui est la sienne mais qui n'est pas celle de l'autre partie,

23 et donc le tribunal doit informer l'autre partie de son droit

24 à un interprète, ce qui a été fait en -- d'entrée de jeu

25 aujourd'hui, mais qui avait également été fait par la Juge...

Briaris Transcription Services

1   l'Honorable Juge Pilon en mars dernier. Monsieur a décliné

2   cette demande d'avoir un interprète. J'attire aussi

3   l'attention --

4   JUDGE THERRIEN: Un instant. Je --

5   MR. DAPONTE: -- du tribunal sur --

6   JUDGE THERRIEN: -- je -- je -- I'm sorry. I -- I --

7   you're saying that Monsieur was provided the possibility to

8   hire an int- an interpreter, but do -- do I understand

9   carefully that the costs of that interpreter is -- is -- is

10 under the -- the -- it's -- it's for the -- Mr. Samuels --

11   MR. DAPONTE: Oui.

12   JUDGE THERRIEN: -- to pay for it and he's not -- he

13 has no resources for that. Is -- is that the situ- --

14   MR. DAPONTE: En fait, le -- la question des

15 ressources n'est pas élaborée dans le procès-verbal que j'ai

16 sous les yeux.

17   JUDGE THERRIEN: Non, non. I'm talking about here,

18 in this precise case. I'm not talking --

19   MR. DAPONTE: Ah, oui.

20   JUDGE THERRIEN: -- I'm not deciding on -- on what

21 happened in the Cour du Québec. I'm -- I -- I will only

22 render a decision in the present case because the issue is

23 raised here in front of me for what I have to do.

24   MR. DAPONTE: Non, je comprends. Excusez-moi de

25 la -- de la méprise.

1   JUDGE THERRIEN: Okay.

2   MR. DAPONTE: Effectivement, je -- je crois

3   comprendre, en tout cas, que... du moins il n'a pas

4   manifesté l'intention de -- de recourir aux services d'un --

5   JUDGE THERRIEN: Okay.

6   MR. DAPONTE: -- interprète pour aujourd'hui.

7   JUDGE THERRIEN: I will just -- I just want to make

8   sure about that. So, Mr. --

9   MR. DAPONTE: Okay.

10   JUDGE THERRIEN: -- Samuels, I want to make sure

11   about one thing. I took for granted that you were offered

12   the possibility to hire int- -- an interpreter, but it has to

13   be paid -- ba- -- paid by yourself. Do I understand

14   carefully that you don't have this kind of money to -- to

15   hire an -- an interpreter? Is that... I don't want to

16   misread your -- your -- your situation.

17   MR. SAMUELS: No, I don't have the resource to

18   hire an interpreter. But I don't -- under -- but -- it --

19   but the -- but my understanding, Your Honour, of the -- of

20   the -- my Charter of Rights is that the -- the court would be

21   providing an interpreter based upon these representations by

22   the court that they -- that section 14 of the Charter is one

23   held by accused persons but -- but also in civil actions and

24   administrative proceedings by the witness -- by the

25   witnesses. And that the Supreme Court of Canada threw out a

1   case because of a refusal to provide an interpreter. So my

2   understanding --

3   JUDGE THERRIEN: Okay.

4   MR. SAMUELS: -- is that the -- that the

5   interpreter is -- that it's -- and that the -- with that in

6   mind, the section 36 of the Quebec Charter of Rights and

7   Freedoms says that -- when it wo- -- when it refers to "Every

8   accused person has the right to be assisted free of charge by

9   an interpreter if he don't -- he does not understand the

10   language used at the hearing or if he is deaf." So that is

11   the -- so section 36 of the -- of the -- is -- of the Quebec

12   Charter of Rights and Freedoms is related to Section 14 of

13   the Canadian Charter of Rights and Freedoms. And the idea

14   that -- that -- that -- that -- that you -- that the only

15   people who can afford int- an interpreter has -- has the

16   right to understand what is going on in a court case. That

17   is unconstitutional to limit the access to the rights to

18   people who have the money to pay for an interpreter.

19   JUDGE THERRIEN: Okay.

20   MR. SAMUELS: That's against the integrity of the

21   Quebec Charter.

22   JUDGE THERRIEN: Okay.

23   MR. SAMUELS: That's against the integrity of the

24   Canadian Charter. And that is something that the Superior

25   Court can consider as a Constitutional Court on whether that

1 it's in fact fair to limit the access to the rights to the

2 people who can afford it.

3   JUDGE THERRIEN: Okay, so it's very clear. Maître

4 Daponte, is there something else you want to add? I'm sorry

5 I've interrupted your... Okay.

6   MR. DAPONTE: Mais ne vous excusez pas. Oui,

7 Madame la Juge, je vais ajouter certains autres éléments. Je

8 constate qu'effectivement que Monsieur réfère à des -- des...

9 des droits qui font référence au -- au droit du... de

10 l'accusé de recourir à des services d'interprètes qui doivent

11 lui être fournis. Cependant, je vous souligne, bien

12 respectueusement, que la situation présente devant vous n'est

13 pas du tout celle d'un accusé. Au contraire, Monsieur est le

14 demandeur dans cette -- dans le litige qui oppose Monsieur à

15 la ville de Gatineau et à ses agents. Au surplus,

16 initialement devant le tribunal des droits de la personne, la

17 commission des droits de la personne et de la jeunesse

18 agitait en faveur de Monsieur. De ce que nous comprenons,

19 elle a cessé d'agir en raison d'un bris quelconque. Monsieur

20 avait aussi la possibilité de se constituer un nouveau

21 procureur, ce qu'il a décliné, ou de se dénicher les services

22 d'un interprète s'il en ressentait le besoin, s'il ne se

23 sentait pas à l'aise de poursuivre son recours seul. Donc, à

24 notre sens, Monsieur avait la possibilité de -- de remédier à

25 la situation qui est la sienne. Puis en tant que demandeur

Briaris Transcription Services

1   spécialement, on ne pense pas que le même type de

2   raisonnement puisse être appliqué à l'encontre de la présente

3   situation.

4   JUDGE THERRIEN: Bien.

5   MR. DAPONTE: Puis en terminant... En fait, j'ai

6   -- j'ai cité l'article 133 de la loi constitutionnelle de

7   1967, mais c'est également des droits qui sont inscrits à

8   l'article 19, par exemple, de la Charte canadienne des droits

9   et libertés, le fait que toute personne peut s'exprimer dans

10 la langue de son choix devant le tribunal -- devant les

11 tribunals canadiens. Donc, le tout respectueusement soumis,

12 je vous remercie de m'avoir écouté.

13   JUDGE THERRIEN: Okay. So, Monsieur Samuels, Maître

14 Daponte only added the -- the -- the specific facts that you

15 were originally in -- in the Cour du Québec -- je -- you were

16 assisted by la commission des droits de la jeunesse, and for

17 some reason that are not explained, you -- they decided not

18 to represent you anymore. You were provided the possibility

19 to hire another lawyer, which you did not use. But, at this

20 point, this -- this situation is not in front of me in -- in

21 the present case. So, at this point, did you -- I understand

22 that you've decided to go on yourself with the procedure. Do

23 you -- do you want to change that decision? Do you wish to

24 have time to have a lawyer to help you in the present case in

25 front of me?

1   MR. SAMUELS: Your Honour, my... Okay, so... The

2 -- the Quebec Human Rights Commission, you know, if -- I'm

3 not sure if Your Honour wants to have that backward or not.

4 But the Quebec --

5   JUDGE THERRIEN: It -- it -- you don't have --

6   MR. SAMUELS: -- Human Rights tr- --

7   JUDGE THERRIEN: Sir, just -- I just want to make

8 sure that -- I want to be clear. You don't have to explain

9 me why --

10   MR. SAMUELS: Okay. Okay.

11   JUDGE THERRIEN: -- you're not represented.

12   MR. SAMUELS: Okay. Okay.

13   JUDGE THERRIEN: It's your total discretion.

14   MR. SAMUELS: Okay.

15   JUDGE THERRIEN: You have the -- the right to

16 represent yourself.

17   MR. SAMUELS: Yes, Your Honour.

18   JUDGE THERRIEN: I just want to make sure that --

19   MR. SAMUELS: Yes?

20   JUDGE THERRIEN: -- if you don't wish to represent

21 yourself, and that you -- you want to change your mind, you

22 want a lawyer, you have the possibility to do so. I just

23 want to -- that's the only point I want to -- to make sure

24 about.

25   MR. SAMUELS: Yes. Thanks for explaining that,

1 Your Honour. Yes, I recognise that right, Your Honour, but I

2 cannot afford $500 an hour and various high expensive lawyers

3 that -- and, you know, based upon what I've been informed

4 [inaudible] I consulted lawyers. They're quite expensive as

5 you can appreciate, Your Honour. But it's my desire, Your

6 Honour, to -- based upon my application to the court, that I

7 would -- I'm seeking for my tr- my case that's currently in

8 the Quebec Human Rights Tribunal, I'm seeking it for it to be

9 transferred to the Quebec Seri- Superior Court, and I've made

10 an application to that. And I'm -- and I'm just getting a

11 bailiff to serve the defendants on my application to transfer

12 from the Quebec Human Rights Tribunal to the Quebec Seri-

13 Superior Court. So that that is my objective, Your Honour.

14   JUDGE THERRIEN: Okay. Okay. So, sir, I want to

15 make sure that you get my decision, which would -- will be

16 written on a paper. So, do we have an email address for you?

17 Do you have an email?

18   MR. SAMUELS: Yes, Your Honour. My -- you have my

19 email address, which is... Well, I believe you would have my

20 email address, but I'll -- I'll give it to you. Should I

21 give it to you, Your Honour?

22   JUDGE THERRIEN: Yes, if you -- if you don't mind.

23 It will be easier for us to deal with that.

24   MR. SAMUELS: So my -- so my email address is Ray,

25 r-a-y --

1   JUDGE THERRIEN: Oops.

2   MR. SAMUELS: -- r-a-y, cosmopolite, c-o-s, m as

3   in mother, o, p as in Peter, o-l-i-t-e --

4   JUDGE THERRIEN: Yeah.

5   MR. SAMUELS: -- at gmail dot com. That's

6   raycosmopolite, one word, at gmail dot com.

7   JUDGE THERRIEN: Okay. So --

8   MR. SAMUELS: But my -- yeah?

9   JUDGE THERRIEN: And your -- your -- your -- on the

10   street address, your physic address, your physical address.

11   Do you have one?

12   MR. SAMUELS: I'm in transit, Your Honour, so I

13   don't --

14   JUDGE THERRIEN: You're in transit?

15   MR. SAMUELS: -- so I believe --

16   JUDGE THERRIEN: Okay.

17   MR. SAMUELS: Yeah, yeah.

18   JUDGE THERRIEN: Okay. So, do you --

19   MR. SAMUELS: So the address that I have would --

20   Yes, Your Honour?

21   JUDGE THERRIEN: -- you have to te- -- to -- to -- to

22   -- to look at your emails often, okay? To make sure --

23   MR. SAMUELS: Yes, your honour.

24   JUDGE THERRIEN: -- that you get my decision, because

25   --

Briaris Transcription Services

1   MR. SAMUELS: Yes, Your Honour.

2   JUDGE THERRIEN: -- you will -- if you want to appeal

3 from -- from my decision, you will need to go -- to address

4 the Court of Appeals. So it's important that you have it in

5 hand. You -- you get me? "In hand," I mean on a written...

6 you -- you need to be able to prove my decision. So you will

7 get it by email. If you want a physical copy, you can come

8 to the clerk's office at the -- the courthouse. I guess

9 that's --

10   MR. SAMUELS: I --

11   JUDGE THERRIEN: -- easy for you.

12   MR. SAMUELS: -- I understand, Your Honour. But I

13 don't understand -- know what we're going to be -- what --

14 what you're deciding on today, because I couldn't understand

15 most of the -- the proceedings today because they were in

16 French.

17   JUDGE THERRIEN: I'm deciding on -- Well, this part,

18 Mr. Samuels, I told you. And I'm speaking --

19   MR. SAMUELS: Yes, Your Honour.

20   JUDGE THERRIEN: -- to you in English. So I've

21 explained it --

22   MR. SAMUELS: Yes, Your Honour.

23   JUDGE THERRIEN: -- to you earlier. I will --

24   MR. SAMUELS: Yes.

25   JUDGE THERRIEN: -- decide on your objection.

1	MR. SAMUELS:	Oh, I see, Your Honour.
2	JUDGE THERRIEN:	Only your objection. I'm not --
3	MR. SAMUELS:	Okay.
4	JUDGE THERRIEN:	-- deciding on what the -- the --

5 the city is asking me. They're -- they're --

6	MR. SAMUELS:	Okay.
7	JUDGE THERRIEN:	-- asking me actually to transfer

8 the -- not -- not to transfer but to decide that I don't have

9 jurisdiction over your -- your -- your -- your so-called

10 appeal, because it has to be sent to the Court of Appeals. I

11 will not decide that. I will just decide on your objection

12 to -- to -- to accept to hear the city's motion since it's

13 only written in French. And I'm not... and I'm not

14 obligating them to speak to you in English. And I'm not

15 providing you translating services. So that's the only issue

16 I will decide.

17	MR. SAMUELS:	Okay, you- --
18	JUDGE THERRIEN:	Basically, it looks --
19	MR. SAMUELS:	Yeah.
20	JUDGE THERRIEN:	-- like this, that what's -- what

21 was decided on the Cour du Québec, but whatever. It's decid-

22 -- you're asking me -- you're -- you're raising an objection,

23 I have to decide on it, okay? And I will decide on it on a

24 written decision. So you will be able to read my decision.

25 And if you want to appeal from that decision, you will have

Briaris Transcription Services

1 to go to the Court of Appeals. But you will have it

2 physically in your hands. But I will send it to you by email

3 since you're transiting from one place to -- to another. I

4 don't know your -- your -- your residence situation, and it's

5 not important at this point since you accept that you will

6 receive it by email.

7   MR. SAMUELS: Okay.

8   JUDGE THERRIEN: Okay?

9   MR. SAMUELS: And will I have it -- will I have an

10 opportunity, Your Honour, of som- of somewhat elaborating on

11 my objection, Your Honour?

12   JUDGE THERRIEN: You want to elaborate more than

13 you've already did?

14   MR. SAMUELS: Well, a little bit. I want to refer

15 to the cases that are the basis of my objection, Your Honour.

16   JUDGE THERRIEN: Okay.

17   MR. SAMUELS: So that your bureau has the

18 reference to that.

19   JUDGE THERRIEN: Okay, no problem. I will give you

20 my own -- my email. So can you send your -- your -- your --

21   MR. SAMUELS: Oh. Oh. I send you [inaudible]

22 email. Okay. Do you want me to email you?

23   JUDGE THERRIEN: If you -- if you want you can --

24   MR. SAMUELS: Yes, okay.

25   JUDGE THERRIEN: -- if you can -- if -- if you prefer

1 to bring me papers, you will have to do it today or at the

2 latest tomorrow. Is it possible?

3   MR. SAMUELS: Okay. Okay. Do you --

4   JUDGE THERRIEN: You can bring it to the clerk's

5 office downstairs, the Palais de Justice?

6   MR. SAMUELS: Do you want to email it to you

7 instead, Your Honour?

8   JUDGE THERRIEN: It's your choice, sir.

9   MR. SAMUELS: O- okay. I can -- I can email, Your

10 Honour.

11   JUDGE THERRIEN: Okay.

12   MR. SAMUELS: I can email it.

13   JUDGE THERRIEN: Okay. Okay. But it has to be

14 before tomorrow at noon. It's possible?

15   MR. SAMUELS: No problem, Your Honour.

16   JUDGE THERRIEN: It's okay?

17   MR. SAMUELS: Yes.

18   JUDGE THERRIEN: And you will have to --

19   MR. SAMUELS: Yes, Your Honour.

20   JUDGE THERRIEN: -- to send a copy to Maître Dupond -

21 - Daponte.

22   MR. SAMUELS: I don't know if I -- I only have

23 Maî- -- Maî- -- Monsieur Turcotte's email.

24   JUDGE THERRIEN: Okay.

25   MR. SAMUELS: And the -- I -- I --

Briaris Transcription Services

1	JUDGE THERRIEN:	Maître Daponte --

2   MR. SAMUELS: -- don't have -- I don't know if I

3 have his email.

4   JUDGE THERRIEN: -- do you prefer that I send it to

5 you?

6   MR. DAPONTE: Please, thank you.

7   JUDGE THERRIEN: Okay. So, Monsieur -- Monsieur

8 Samuels, if you --

9   MR. SAMUELS: Yes, Your Honour?

10   JUDGE THERRIEN: -- don't mind -- Samuels, sorry.

11   MR. SAMUELS: Yeah.

12   JUDGE THERRIEN: Once you send it to me, I will just

13 send a copy to Maître Daponte. That's fine with you?

14   MR. SAMUELS: Okay, Your Honour.

15   JUDGE THERRIEN: Okay.

16   MR. SAMUELS: Okay, Your Honour.

17   JUDGE THERRIEN: So it's less trouble for you and the

18 --

19   MR. SAMUELS: Okay.

20   JUDGE THERRIEN: -- job will be done, okay?

21   MR. SAMUELS: Okay.

22   JUDGE THERRIEN: Okay. Okay, so I give you my email

23 and it's only for that purpose. You don't send me anything

24 else.

25   MR. SAMUELS: Yes, Your Honour.

1	JUDGE THERRIEN:	Okay.
2	MR. SAMUELS:	No, no, Your Honour.
3	JUDGE THERRIEN:	Okay.
4	MR. SAMUELS:	Okay, Your Honour.
5	JUDGE THERRIEN:	So, it's Carole, c-a-r- --
6	MR. SAMUELS:	C-a-r.
7	JUDGE THERRIEN:	-- o-l-e --
8	MR. SAMUELS:	O-l-e.
9	JUDGE THERRIEN:	Yeah. Dot --
10	MR. SAMUELS:	Dot.
11	JUDGE THERRIEN:	-- Therrien, t-h-e-r-r-i-e-n, as in
12	Nicole --	
13	MR. SAMUELS:	Huh-huh.
14	JUDGE THERRIEN:	-- at g-e-d- -- no, sorry. I made a
15	mistake. G-u-d --	
16	MR. SAMUELS:	G -- just sorry. G-u-d.
17	JUDGE THERRIEN:	-- d --
18	MR. SAMUELS:	What's the --
19	JUDGE THERRIEN:	G --
20	MR. SAMUELS:	G-u-d.
21	JUDGE THERRIEN:	G-u-d-e --
22	MR. SAMUELS:	Yeah.
23	JUDGE THERRIEN:	-- x.
24	MR. SAMUELS:	G-u-d-e-x, yeah.
25	JUDGE THERRIEN:	-- do- -- d, dot q-c dot c-a.

Briaris Transcription Services

1   MR. SAMUELS: Sorry, your Honor. Sorry, Your

2   Honour. G-u-d-e-x point --

3   JUDGE THERRIEN: Dot.

4   MR. SAMUELS: -- dot, and what?

5   JUDGE THERRIEN: -- dot q-c- --

6   MR. SAMUELS: Q-c?

7   JUDGE THERRIEN: -- dot c-a.

8   MR. SAMUELS: Dot c-a.

9   JUDGE THERRIEN: Yeah. So that's it.

10   MR. SAMUELS: C-a -- c-a-r-o-l-e dot t-h-e-r-r-i-

11 e-n at g-u-d-e-x dot q-c dot c-a.

12   JUDGE THERRIEN: That's it.

13   MR. SAMUELS: Okay, then.

14   JUDGE THERRIEN: Okay.

15   MR. SAMUELS: So I send it there. Okay.

16   JUDGE THERRIEN: Okay. So -- so, Madame la

17 Greffière?

18   THE CLERK: Oui.

19   JUDGE THERRIEN: Le tribunal -- "The -- the court

20 grants that -- the -- the applicant 24 hours to send

21 jurisprudence to the undersigned, and the court will send the

22 jurisprudence to the defendants' attorney." Okay. And "The

23 court" -- paragraphe,

24   "The court takes under advisement Mr. Samuels's

25 objection and advise the parties that judgment will be sent

1 by email to the parties." Paragraphe.

2   "Meanwhile, the file is suspended until judgment is

3 rendered." That's it. Okay? So, that's all for today, Mr.

4 Samuels. Thank you for your presence. I will render my

5 judgment, and you will see what you have to do after that.

6 Oops. Are you there?

7   MR. SAMUELS: Yes. So...

8   JUDGE THERRIEN: Okay.

9   MR. SAMUELS: So... so after you suspend it,

10 so... "suspended." What does --

11   JUDGE THERRIEN: C'est -- It means --

12   MR. SAMUELS: -- suspended mean? Can you clarify

13 that, Your Honour?

14   JUDGE THERRIEN: It's just -- it means that the --

15 the delays are not running. So it's like frozen until my

16 judgment is rendered.

17   MR. SAMUELS: Mh'mh. Mh'mh. Mh'.

18   JUDGE THERRIEN: But you may -- you -- if you have

19 things to -- to -- to bring to the court's -- to the court --

20 the clerk's office, you can -- you can. It's not a problem.

21   MR. SAMUELS: Mh'mh. Mh'mh. Mh'mh.

22   JUDGE THERRIEN: Okay?

23   MR. SAMUELS: Oh, okay then. So -- and you'll be

24 sending through -- and you -- and you'll be making a

25 decision...

Briaris Transcription Services

```
1        JUDGE THERRIEN:     It will be fast.

2        MR. SAMUELS:        Did you...

3        JUDGE THERRIEN:     It will be fast.

4        MR. SAMUELS:        Oh, okay.

5        JUDGE THERRIEN:     Not more than --

6        MR. SAMUELS:        Okay, Your Honour.

7        JUDGE THERRIEN:     -- a few days.

8        MR. SAMUELS:        Okay then.

9        JUDGE THERRIEN:     Okay?

10       MR. SAMUELS:        Okay, Your Honour.  Okay, Your

11  Honour.  So I'll send this representation to you.

12       JUDGE THERRIEN:     Oh okay, thank you.  Have a good

13  day.

14       MR. SAMUELS:        Okay, Your Honour.  Thank you, Your

15  Honour.

16       JUDGE THERRIEN:     You're welcome.

17       MR. DAPONTE:        Merci.  Bonne journée à vous.  Au

18  revoir.

19       JUDGE THERRIEN:     Merci à vous.  Thank you, goodbye.

20

21  ...END OF PROCEEDING.
```

Briaris Transcription Services

CERTIFICATE OF COURT TRANSCRIBER

I, Brian Fino, Court Transcriber, hereby certify that I have transcribed the foregoing and that it is a true and accurate transcript of the evidence given in the matter, taken by way of electronic tape recording.

June 23, 2023

PROCÈS-VERBAL (suite)

	Date du jour			Numéro du dossier						
	A	M	J						Page 1	de 14
	2023	03	15	550	53	000051	22	0		

CANADA
PROVINCE DE QUÉBEC
District : Gatineau

TRIBUNAL DES DROITS DE LA PERSONNE

PROCÈS-VERBAL

IDENTIFICATION

	Date			Numéro du dossier				
	2023	03	15	550	53	000051	22	0

Nature	Salle
Conférence de gestion	

HEURES D'AUDIENCE	DÉBUT 9h54	FIN 11h13	DÉBUT	FIN

JUGE	**CATHERINE PILON**	Code JP2379
ASSESSEUR(E)		
ASSESSEUR(E)		

GREFFIER(E)-AUDIENCIER(ÈRE)   Joseth Etienne, g.a.c.Q.

RAYMOND SAMUELS *partie demanderesse*	**NON-REPRÉSENTÉ (P)**
VILLE DE GATINEAU -et- **MATHIEU BRAZEAU** -et- **GUILLAUME CHOQUETTE BUSSIÈRE** -et- **JONATHAN DESJARDINS** -et- **NICOLAS GAGNON** -et- **SHAWN MAHAR** *parties défenderesses*	Me Mathieu Turcotte (P) **DHC AVOCATS INC.** *pour la défenderesse*
RAYMOND SAMUELS *partie plaignante*	
CENTRE RECHERCHE ACTION SUR LES RELATIONS RACIALES *partie organisme plaignant*	

REMARQUES : *Gestion*

HEURES	
9h54	Identification de la cause et de M. Raymond Samuels et de Me Mathieu Turcotte
9h54	Le Tribunal s'adresse aux parties.

PROCÈS-VERBAL (suite)	Date du jour A M J 2 0 2 3 | 03 | 1 5	Numéro du dossier 550 | 53 | 000051 | 22 | 0 Page 2 de 14

9h59	M. Samuels indique au Tribunal que pour le moment il ne sera pas représenté par avocat et demande au Tribunal quelles règles de procédure qu'il doit suivre pour la suite des événements. Le Tribunal lui mentionne qu'il doit suivre les mêmes règles de procédures que s'il était représenté par avocat et qu'il ne peut lui prodiguer de conseils.
	Le Tribunal explique par ailleurs à M. Samuels que du temps d'audience au fond avait été indiqué par la CDPDJ pour trois jours du côté de la demande et de trois jours du côté de la défense pour l'audience au fond.
	M. Samuels indique qu'un interrogatoire préalable a eu lieu pour lequel divers documents ont été demandés alors qu'il était encore représenté par la CDPDJ. Me Turcotte informe le Tribunal que certains de ces documents ont fait l'objet d'objections sous réserve qui doivent être débattues. M. Samuels s'oppose quant à lui à toutes les demandes de documents car il les considère toutes en violation de ses droits.
	Il appert donc nécessaire au Tribunal de fixer une date et pour le débat des objections et pour que M. Samuels puisse expliquer en quoi les autres demandes sont à son avis irrecevables.
	M.Samuels souligne qu'il exige que Me Turcotte parle anglais. Le Tribunal lui explique que Me Turcotte n'a pas cette obligation ni le Tribunal, quoiqu'il lui parle anglais par courtoisie. Le Tribunal souligne également à M. Samuels qu'il n'agit pas comme interprète. Si M. Samuels souhaite avoir un interprète, il devra en requérir les services.
	M. Samuels dit qu'il n'a pas de copie de la transcription de son interrogatoire. Cependant, questionné par le Tribunal, il admet que la CDPDJ lui a fourni une copie de son dossier lorsqu'elle a cessé de le représenter. Le Tribunal lui suggère de regarder le dossier et qu'une copie de son interrogatoire doit s'y retrouver.

PROCÈS-VERBAL (suite)

Date du jour			Numéro du dossier						Page		
A	M	J									
2 0 2 3	03	15	550	53	000051	22	0		3	de	14

Le Tribunal est d'avis qu'une journée complète sera nécessaire pour entendre les demandes des parties soient :

    - Trancher les objections de l'interrogatoire de la partie de demanderesse du 21 décembre 2022;

    - Le refus général de la partie demanderesse de fournir les engagements auxquels il n'y a pas eu d'objection.

Le Tribunal a vérifié auprès du greffe et la juge soussignée pourra entendre le débat sur les objections et la production des documents et la demande de rejet de la défense les 6 ou 13 octobre prochain. Me Turcotte sera en procès, mais s'engage à confier le dossier à un de ses collègues afin qu'il puisse procéder. Le Tribunal avait également proposé les dates des 19 avril, 10 mai et 7 juin pour rôle de gestion. Cependant, les parties n'étaient pas disponibles.

M. Samuels se dit maintenant disponible le 19 avril, mais le Tribunal lui explique que la durée nécessaire pour entendre toutes les demandes requerra une journée complète et qu'il n'est pas approprié de fixer les demandes de gestion de l'instance au 19 avril prochain sur le rôle de gestion habituel.

M. Samuels souhaite que la demande de rejet de la défense sur une base sommaire qu'il annonce vouloir présenter soit entendue séparément avant le 6 octobre. Le Tribunal lui explique toutefois qu'il est dans l'intérêt de la justice que toutes les demandes soient entendues ensemble en une même journée.

Le Tribunal rappelle à M. Samuels l'article 228 (2) du *Code de procédure civile* relativement aux motifs qui peuvent permettre de refuser de répondre à une question lors d'un interrogatoire préalable et de soulever une objection.

Le Tribunal rappelle aussi M. Samuels que s'il souhaite avoir les services d'un interprète il doit les réserver lui-même et en payer les frais ou qu'il peut aussi être aidé par une personne qui parle français.

M. Samuels réitère qu'il souhaite que sa demande pour jugement sommaire, comme il l'a qualifiée, soit entendue avant le 6 octobre. Le Tribunal lui répète que cette demande sera entendue le 6 octobre prochain.

PROCÈS-VERBAL (suite)	Date du jour			Numéro du dossier						
	A	M	J							Page 4 de 14
	2023	03	15	550	53	000051	22	0		

M. Samuels s'engage à produire sa demande écrite pour rejet du mémoire des parties défenderesses d'ici le 15 juin 2023. Le Tribunal lui rappelle qu'il devra déposer sa demande au greffe à Gatineau et qu'il n'aura pas besoin d'y indiquer une date de présentation. Puisqu'elle est déjà déterminée pour le 6 octobre 2023.

Me Turcotte s'engage à produire un tableau des objections d'ici le 15 juin 2023 avec une transcription de l'interrogatoire. Il aimerait aussi présenter une demande de rejet pour avoir fait défaut de fournir les engagements lors de l'audience du 6 octobre. Le Tribunal est plutôt d'avis que cette demande est prématurée à ce stade et qu'elle pourra, si nécessaire, être entendue à un moment à être fixé après le 6 octobre.

Le Tribunal demande à M. Samuels de produire une courte argumentation indiquant pourquoi il conteste les demandes d'engagement qui n'ont pas fait l'objet d'objection. M. Samuels refuse de le faire dans ce délai, car il considère que cela donnera trop de temps aux parties défenderesses. Le Tribunal estime juste que M. Samuels produise son argumentation dans ce délai.

La juge soussignée reste saisie du dossier pour les fins de l'audience du 6 octobre 2023.

POUR CES MOTIFS, LE TRIBUNAL :

FIXE au 6 octobre 2023 pour une journée une audience sur les demandes interlocutoires suivantes :

- Débat sur les objections soulevées par la partie demanderesse lors de l'interrogatoire du 21 décembre 2022;

- Débat sur le refus de la partie demanderesse de fournir les engagements pour lesquels il n'y a pas eu d'objection;

- Demande de la partie demanderesse en rejet sommaire du mémoire des parties défenderesses.

PROCÈS-VERBAL (suite)	Date du jour			Numéro du dossier					

	ORDONNE aux parties défenderesses de produire d'ici le 15 juin 2023 un tableau des objections à débattre et une transcription de l'interrogatoire;
	ORDONNE aux parties défenderesses de produire une transcription de l'interrogatoire;
	ORDONNE à la partie demanderesse de produire d'ici le 15 juin 2023 sa demande pour rejet du mémoire des parties défenderesses et une courte argumentation expliquant son refus de fournir les engagements requis à la suite de son interrogatoire du 21 décembre 2022 pour lesquels qu'il n'y avait pas eu d'objection.
	_____ Catherine Pilon Juge au Tribunal des droits de la personne
10h57	Le Tribunal souligne que tout ce qui précède a été expliqué en anglais à M. Samuels
10h17	**SUSPENSION DE LA CONFÉRENCE DE GESTION**
10h29	**REPRISE DE LA CONFÉRENCE DE GESTION**
11h02	**SUSPENSION DE LA CONFÉRENCE DE GESTION**
11h08	**REPRISE DE LA CONFÉRENCE DE GESTION**
11h09	M. Samuels soulève qu'il croit que la juge soussignée ne peut rester saisie du dossier et indique qu'il a l'intention de demander sa récusation. Il dit avoir des motifs mais qu'il n'est pas prêt à les donner aujourd'hui. À tout événement, le Tribunal lui explique que la demande de récusation doit être entendue par la juge soussignée conformément à l'article 205 du _Code de procédure civile_ et qu'il doit invoquer les motifs prévus à de l'article 202 du _Code de procédure civile_. De plus, sa demande doit être faite par écrit. Elle sera entendue en début d'audience le 6 octobre 2023. **POUR CES MOTIFS, LE TRIBUNAL :** ORDONNE à M. Samuels de produire une demande écrite justifiant ses motifs de récusation de la juge soussignée, appuyée d'une déclaration sous serment, d'ici le 15 juin 2023. _____ Catherine Pilon Juge au Tribunal des droits de la personne

PROCÈS-VERBAL (suite)		Date du jour			Numéro du dossier						
		A	M	J							Page 6 de 14
		2 0 2 3	03	15	550	53	000051	22	0		
	Le Tribunal souligne que tout ce qui précède a été expliqué en anglais à M. Samuels										
	NOTE : L'ordre des discussions survenues lors de la conférence de gestion a été modifié, lors de la rédaction du procès-verbal, afin d'en faciliter la lecture.										
11h13	Fin de la conférence de gestion										
	Joseth Etienne, g.a.C.Q.										

SA MAJESTÉ LE ROI

CANADA

PROVINCE DU QUÉBEC

Dossier No. 550-53-000051-220

P R O C É D U R E S

DEVANT L'HONORABLE JUGE CATHERINE PILON

LE 15 MARS 2023

PRÉSENCES :

M. R. Samuels   Pour la Couronne

Me. Turcotte   Pour l'accusé

Briaris Transcription Services

TABLE DES MATIÈRES

DATE DE LA TRANSCRIPTION : Le 8 avril 2023

DATE DE LA TRANSCRIPTION REQUISE : Le 8 avril 2023

1   [00:00:00] GREFFIÈRE DE LA COUR: Donc, j'appelle le

2   dossier de la Commission des droits de la personne et des

3   droits de la jeunesse agissant dans un intérêt public et en

4   faveur de Raymond Samuels contre Ville de Gatineau, Mathieu

5   Brazeau, contre Guillaume Choquette-Bussière, contre Jonathan

6   Desjardins, contre Nicolas Gagnon, contre Shawn Mahar.

7   Maître, identifiez-vous s'il --

8   [00:00:24] LE TRIBUNAL: J'aurais besoin du dossier,

9   Madame Étienne.

10   [00:00:26] GREFFIÈRE DE LA COUR: Pas de soucis.

11   [00:00:27] LE TRIBUNAL: Dossier 4.

12

13   [ANGLAIS]

14

15   [00:05:48] LE TRIBUNAL: Madame Étienne, si vous voulez

16   le noter "Le --

17

18   [ANGLAIS]

19

20   [00:06:54] LE TRIBUNAL: Madame Étienne, notez que "Le -

21   - la partie plaignante -- " en fait, ce n'est pas la partie

22   plaignante, excusez-moi. "Le... le -- la partie

23   demanderesse indique au tribunal que pour le moment il ne

24   sera pas représenté par avocat et il demande au tribunal

25   quelles règles de procédure il doit suivre pour la suite des

1 événements. Le tribunal lui indique qu'il doit suivre les

2 règles de procédure comme s'il était représenté par avocat et

3 qu'il ne peut lui prodiguer de conseils.

4   Le tribunal lui explique par -- Le tribunal explique par

5 ailleurs à la partie demanderesse que du temps d'audience

6 avait été indiqué pour trois jours du côté de la demande et

7 trois jours du côté de la défense."

8

9   [ANGLAIS]

10

11   [00:09:21] ME. TURCOTTE: Il y avait, Madame la Juge,

12 plusieurs objections sous réserve. En fait, plusieurs

13 réserves effectivement. Je suis en train de passer la liste

14 des engagements. Il y a neuf engagements qui ont été

15 souscrits, dont plusieurs l'ont été sans aucune réserve,

16 notamment, Madame la Juge. Et je suspecte que ça fait partie

17 du -- du cœur de la contestation, notamment les... le

18 dossier médical du... de la -- du demandeur, parce qu'il y a

19 des allégations concernant les impacts médicaux sur sa santé

20 en lien avec la situation qui fait l'objet de la plainte. Il

21 y a eu une demande d'engagement. Monsieur a fait des

22 commentaires en interrogatoire et la -- la procureure de la

23 Commission lui a expliqué en interrogatoire qu'il avait

24 l'obligation de fournir ce documents-là. C'est un exemple

25 mais c'est probablement ce qui est au cœur du litige. Alors,

57

1   pour le reste, il y a certains engagements qui ont été

2   souscrits sous réserve. Ce qui fait que il y a deux choses

3   qui peuvent se produire. On va devoir faire trancher ces

4   objections préalablement --

5   [00:10:29] LE TRIBUNAL: Oui.

6   [00:10:20] ME. TURCOTTE: -- et où je -- j'avise la -- la

7   Cour que j'ai l'intention de demander le rejet de la demande

8   dans la mesure où Monsieur refuse de fournir les documents

9   qu'il a souscrit en engagement.

10   [00:10:30] LE TRIBUNAL: Il va falloir d'abord faire --

11 il va falloir d'abord trancher les objections, je pense avant

12 de pouvoir... et là vous verrez qu'est-ce que --

13   [00:10:36] ME. TURCOTTE: Pour --

14   [00:10:37] LE TRIBUNAL: -- à -- ce quoi on -- ce qui

15 est accordé, ce qui n'est pas accordé et -- et -- et... et

16 après ça vous verrez.

17   [00:10:44] ME. TURCOTTE: -- pour ceux qui font l'objet

18 d'une objection -- oui, c'est ça, pour ceux qui font l'objet

19 d'une objection je comprends bien que c'est comme ça que ça

20 doit se passer. Pour ceux qui ne font pas l'objet d'une

21 objection et pour lequel je comprends ce matin qu'il y a un

22 refus, à mon sens, on en est à l'étape à demander -- de

23 demander le rejet de la demande à ce titre là, mais ceci

24 étant dit pratico-pratique le tout devra probablement se

25 faire au cours de la même audience, j'en suis bien conscient.

1

2   [ANGLAIS]

3

4   [00:13:23] LE TRIBUNAL: Madame Étienne, oubliez la

5 question des pièces. On va plutôt indiquer "Le -- la partie

6 demanderesse indique qu'un interrogatoire préalable a eu lieu

7 pour lequel divers documents ont été demandés." "A eu lieu,"

8 vous mettrez "alors qu'il était encore représenté par la...

9 la CDPDJ, pour lequel divers documents ont été demandés.

10 Maître Turcotte informe le tribunal que certains de ces

11 documents ont fait l'objet d'une objection sous réserve qui

12 doit être... on fait l'objet d'objections sous réserve qui

13 doivent être débattues. La partie demanderesse indique quant

14 à lui s'opposer à toutes les demandes de documents qu'il

15 considère en violation de ses droits.

16   Il apparaît donc nécessaire au tribunal de fixer une

17 date pour le débat des objections et pour que Monsieur --

18 pour que la partie demanderesse puisse indiquer en quoi les

19 autres demandes sont à son avis irrecevables."

20

21   [ANGLAIS]

22

23   [00:16:07] ME. TURCOTTE: Vous avez mentionné le 19

24 avril, Madame la Juge. C'est bien ça ?

25   [00:16:10] LE TRIBUNAL: Oui. 10 mai, 7 juin. Alors,

1   Madame Étienne ?

2   [00:16:13] ME. TURCOTTE: Moi le 19 --

3   [00:16:16] LE TRIBUNAL: Oui. Juste un instant. "La

4   partie demanderesse souligne que -- qu'il exige que Maître

5   Turcotte parle anglais. Le tribunal lui explique que Maître

6   Turcotte n'a pas cette obligation, ni le tribunal quoi qu'il

7   lui parle anglais par courtoisie. Le tribunal souligne

8   également à Monsieur -- " ou " -- à la partie demanderesse

9   qu'il n'agit pas comme interprète. Si la partie demanderesse

10 souhaite avoir un interprète, il devra en requérir les

11 services."

12

13   [ANGLAIS]

14

15   [00:17:14] ME. TURCOTTE: En ce qui me concerne le 19

16 avril est la seule date qui fonctionne, et je suis en

17 interrogatoire et en audience les autres dates.

18   [00:17:20] LE TRIBUNAL: Okay.

19

20   [ANGLAIS]

21

22   [00:17:57] LE TRIBUNAL: En fait, pouvez-vous appeler ?

23

24   [ANGLAIS]

25

1   [00:18:32] LE TRIBUNAL: Bon... Alors, date à fixer.

2   [00:18:40] ME. TURCOTTE: Madame la Juge, --

3   [00:18:41] LE TRIBUNAL: Oui ?

4   [00:18:41] ME. TURCOTTE: -- je dois juste souligner au

5   tribunal que j'ai à partir du mois de septembre ça va être

6   extrêmement difficile en ce qui me concerne. Je vais devoir

7   demander à un collègue. Je vais être en procès pendant sept

8   semaines à Québec à partir du 11 septembre, alors ça va -- ça

9   va être très difficile. Si jamais la Cour a d'autres dates

10   avant les vacances, ça serait idéal.

11   [00:19:01] LE TRIBUNAL: Non. On fait une -- une --

12   [00:19:03] ME. TURCOTTE: Non ?

13   [00:19:03] LE TRIBUNAL: -- on fait une pratique par --

14   par mois, une journée de pratique par mois.

15   [00:19:08] ME. TURCOTTE: D'accord.

16   [00:19:09] LE TRIBUNAL: Alors...

17

18   [ANGLAIS]

19

20   [00:19:25] ME. TURCOTTE: Oui, je vais demander -- je

21   vais devoir demander un remplacement, effectivement, oui.

22

23   [ANGLAIS]

24

25   [00:23:32] LE TRIBUNAL: Je sais Maître Turcotte que

1 vous -- vous avez des gens qui attendent après vous, mais

2 moi, c'est parce que j'aimerais ça de --

3

4   [ANGLAIS]

5

6   [00:23:52] LE TRIBUNAL: Alors, Madame Étienne, on va

7 suspendre s'il vous plaît. Je vais appeler Madame Robbie

8 (ph).

9   [00:23:58] GREFFIÈRE DE LA COUR: Veuillez-vous lever,

10 demeurez à vos places. Comme séance au tribunal des droits

11 de la personne est suspendue.

12

13   (BRÈVE SUSPENSION DE SÉANCE)

14

15   [ANGLAIS]

16

17   [00:36:34] ME. TURCOTTE: Je vais lui envoyer la

18 transcription sténographique, Madame la Juge.

19

20   [ANGLAIS]

21

22   [00:36:52] LE TRIBUNAL: Une copie papier ou

23 électronique, Maître Turcotte?

24   [00:36:55] ME. TURCOTTE: Électronique. Je -- je présume

25 par ailleurs, je ne connais pas la -- la procédure, mais que

1 quand la Commission a cessé d'occuper, ils ont dû remettre un

2 dossier à Monsieur Samuels [inaudible] ?

3   [00:37:04] LE TRIBUNAL: Ça, je pourrais pas vous dire.

4

5   [ANGLAIS]

6

7   [00:37:45] LE TRIBUNAL: -- Maitre des rôles --

8

9   [ANGLAIS]

10

11   [00:38:04] LE TRIBUNAL: Alors, Madame Étienne, on va --

12

13   [ANGLAIS]

14

15   [00:38:09] LE TRIBUNAL: Et puis, Maître Turcotte, je ne

16 sais pas si ça va marcher dans votre horaire, sinon je vous

17 demanderai d'avoir un de vos collègues pour qu'on puisse

18 avancer un peu avec le dossier.

19

20   [ANGLAIS]

21

22   [00:38:30] ME. TURCOTTE: En ce qui me concerne dans les

23 deux cas, comme je vous ai mentionné, je vais être à -- à

24 Québec, mais... je vais laisser Monsieur Samuels vous

25 mentionner s'il est disponible.

63

Briaris Transcription Services

1

2   [ANGLAIS]

3

4   [00:39:03] LE TRIBUNAL: Madame Étienne, notez que
5   "Le... la partie demanderesse indique qu'il n'a pas de
6   copies de la transcription de son interrogatoire. Cependant,
7   questionné par le tribunal il admet que la CDPDJ lui a fourni
8   une copie son dossier lorsqu'elle a cessé de le représenter.
9   Le tribunal lui indique qu'une copie de son interrogatoire
10   doit s'y retrouver." Alors...   "Après vérification avec les
11   parties --
12   "Le tribunal est d'avis qu'une journée complète sera
13   nécessaire pour entendre les demandes des parties soit :
14   - trancher les objections de l'interrogatoire de la
15   partie demanderesse du -- " c'était quelle date
16   l'interrogatoire, Maître Turcotte ?
17   [00:40:33] ME. TURCOTTE: En décembre... le 21 décembre
18   2022.
19   [00:40:41] LE TRIBUNAL: " -- du -- du 21 décembre 2022
20   - Le refus général du -- de la partie demanderesse de
21   fournir les engagements auxquels il n'y a pas eu
22   d'objections." Et --

23

24   [ANGLAIS]

25

11

64

Briaris Transcription Services

1   [00:41:30] LE TRIBUNAL: Alors, "La demande du demandeur

2 de rejeter --

3

4   [ANGLAIS]

5

6   [00:44:37] LE TRIBUNAL: Alors, Madame Étienne,

7 "Monsieur -- le -- la partie deman- Alors, "Le tribunal a

8 vérifié auprès du greffe et la Juge soussignée pourra

9 entendre le débat sur les objections et la production des

10 documents et la demande de rejet de la défense les 6 ou 13

11 octobre prochains. Maître Turcotte sera en procès mais

12 s'engage à confier le dossier à un de ses collègues afin

13 qu'il puisse procéder." Et vous mettrez quand -- quand j'ai

14 parlé des dates du... " -- procéder. Le tribunal a -- avait

15 également proposé les dates des 19 avril, 10 mai et 7 juin au

16 rôle de gestion cependant les parties n'étaient pas

17 disponible. La partie demanderesse se dit maintenant

18 disponible le 19 avril mais le tribunal lui explique que la

19 durée nécessaire pour entendre toutes les demandes requerra

20 une journée complète et qu'il n'est pas approprié de fixer au

21 -- les demandes au rôle de gestion de l'instance du 19 avril.

22 Le dem- la partie demanderesse indique également qu'il

23 souhaite que sa demande de rejet soit entendue séparément

24 avant le 6 octobre mais le tribunal lui indique qu'il est

25 dans l'intérêt de la justice que toutes les demandes soient

Briaris Transcription Services

1   entendues ensemble en une même journée.

2

3   [ANGLAIS]

4

5   [00:47:42] LE TRIBUNAL: Alors, Madame Étienne, "Le

6   tribunal rappelle à la partie demanderesse l'article 228.2 -

7   " donc, "(228.2 du code de procédure civile) relativement aux

8   motifs qui peuvent permettre de refuser de répondre à une

9   question lors d'un interrogatoire préalable."

10

11   [ANGLAIS]

12

13   [00:48:48] LE TRIBUNAL: Okay. "Le tribunal --

14   "Le tribunal rappelle aussi à la partie demanderesse que

15   s'il souhaite avoir les services d'un interprète il doit les

16   réserver lui-même et en payer les frais mais qu'il peut aussi

17   être aidé par une personne qui parle français pour les fins

18   de l'audience."

19   [00:49:15] ME. TURCOTTE: Madame la Juge, --

20   [00:49:16] LE TRIBUNAL: Oui ?

21   [00:49:16] ME. TURCOTTE: -- si vous me permettez, je --

22   je pense qu'il serait approprié de fixer des dates pour

23   déposer toutes les demandes --

24   [00:49:21] LE TRIBUNAL: Oui, je --

25   [00:49:21] ME. TURCOTTE: -- écrites [inaudible].

1   [00:49:22] LE TRIBUNAL: -- oui, oui. Je n'étais pas

2   encore rendu là, mais ça faisait partie du plan, okay ?

3   [00:49:26] ME. TURCOTTE: Parfait merci.

4   [00:49:27] LE TRIBUNAL: Bien.

5

6   [ANGLAIS]

7

8   [00:51:04] LE TRIBUNAL: Madame Étienne, "Le -- La

9   partie demanderesse réitère qu'il souhaite maintenant que la

10   -- sa demande pour jugement sommaire, comme il la qualifie,

11   soit entendue avant le 6 octobre."

12

13   [ANGLAIS]

14

15   [00:51:42] LE TRIBUNAL: "Le tribunal lui indique à

16   nouveau que la demande -- cette demande sera entendue le 6

17   octobre."

18

19   [ANGLAIS]

20

21   [00:53:59] LE TRIBUNAL: Alors, "Le demand- --

22   [00:54:00] ME. TURCOTTE: Ma- Ma- --

23   [00:54:01] LE TRIBUNAL: Oui ? Oui ?

24   [00:54:02] ME. TURCOTTE: Madame la -- Madame la --

25   Madame la Juge, par contre là, je vais confier ça à un

1 collègue, mais avant de confier ça à un collègue, j'aimerais

2 quand même avoir l'opportunité de la -- de la lire et puis de

3 la comprendre sa requête parce que pour l'instant je ne la

4 comprends pas. Je demanderai quand même qu'on -- que -- que

5 la requête soit déposée de façon écrite avant l'été, pour que

6 on puisse s'organiser en conséquence au bureau. Je ne peux

7 pas confier à n'importe qui en fonction de ce qu'il y a dans

8 la requête. Je pense que --

9   [00:54:23] LE TRIBUNAL: Bon.

10   [00:54:23] ME. TURCOTTE: -- c'est raisonnable de -- de -

11 -

12   [00:54:24] LE TRIBUNAL: Okay.

13   [00:54:25] ME. TURCOTTE: -- de donner le délai de... je

14 sais pas, un mois ou deux au plaignant pour faire sa -- sa

15 demande écrite.

16

17   [ANGLAIS]

18

19   [00:55:24] LE TRIBUNAL: Alors, "Le -- La partie

20 demanderesse s'engage à produire sa demande écrite pour rejet

21 du mémoire des défendre- de la partie -- des parties

22 défenderesses d'ici le 15 juin 2023."

23

24   [ANGLAIS]

25

1   [00:55:51] LE TRIBUNAL: "Le tribunal lui rappelle qu'il

2 devra --

3

4   [ANGLAIS]

5

6   [00:56:01] LE TRIBUNAL: "Le tribunal lui rappelle qu'il

7 devra déposer sa demande au greffe à Gatineau et qu'il n'aura

8 pas besoin d'indiquer une date de présentation.

9

10   [ANGLAIS]

11

12   [00:56:32] LE TRIBUNAL: Ensuite --

13

14   [ANGLAIS]

15

16   [00:56:46] LE TRIBUNAL: Maître Turcotte, de votre côté

17 le tableau des objections. Pouvez-vous nous faire ça --

18   [00:56:53] ME. TURCOTTE: Ça -- ça peut être fait oui

19 d'ici --

20   [00:56:54] LE TRIBUNAL: -- pour le 15 juin?

21   [00:56:55] ME. TURCOTTE: -- un mois. Oh, même délai,

22 pas -- pas de problème.

23   [00:56:58] LE TRIBUNAL: Le même délai. Okay. Alors,

24 "Maître Turcotte s'engage à produire un tableau des

25 objections d'ici le 15 juin 2023 avec une transcription de

1   l'interrogatoire."

2   [00:57:18] ME. TURCOTTE: Oui.

3

4   [ANGLAIS]

5

6   [00:57:21] ME. TURCOTTE: Le script complet.

7   [00:57:23] LE TRIBUNAL: Oui.

8

9   [ANGLAIS]

10

11   [00:57:42] LE TRIBUNAL: "Le tribunal --

12

13   [ANGLAIS]

14

15   [00:58:35] LE TRIBUNAL: Alors, Madame Étienne, "Le

16   tribunal demande à Monsieur Samuels de produire une courte

17   argumentation indiquant pourquoi il conteste les demandes de

18   prod- les demandes d'engagement qui n'ont pas fait l'objet

19   d'objections. Monsieur Samuels refuse de le faire dans ce

20   délai car il considère que cela donnerait trop de temps aux

21   parties défenderesses. Le tribunal est d'avis -- Le tribunal

22   estime juste que Monsieur Samuels -- que la -- la partie

23   demanderesse -- " on mettra peut-être Monsieur Samuels dans

24   le procès-verbal, on verra, Madame Étienne, on va s'en

25   reparler. " -- produise son argumentation dans ce délai."

1   Alors, "Pour ces motifs le tribunal -- " non, avant de mettre

2   ça, vous mettrez "La juge soussignée reste saisi du dossier

3   pour les fins de l'audience du 6 octobre 2023. Pour ces

4   motifs le tribunal fixe au 6 octobre 2023 pour une journée

5   une audience sur les demandes interlocutoires suivantes :

6   débat sur les objections -- " et Maître, vous allez recevoir

7   une copie de mon procès-verbal, soyez sans crainte, " --

8   débat sur les objections soulevé lors de l'interrogatoire du

9   -- " on avait quelle date ? En décembre 2022, Maître

10   Turcotte ?

11   [01:00:49] ME. TURCOTTE: 21 décembre 2022.

12   [01:00:49] LE TRIBUNAL: " -- du 21 décembre 2022."

13   [01:00:58] ME. TURCOTTE: Une demande incidente en rejet,

14   Madame la Juge. Je -- je le précise pour ce qui est des

15   objections à tout le moment qui ne font pas l'objet d'une...

16   pas des objections, des engagements qui ne font pas l'objet

17   d'une objection.

18   [01:01:11] LE TRIBUNAL: Non. On va commencer, Maître

19   Turcotte, par entendre ce que Monsieur a à dire là-dessus et

20   puis on verra après.

21   [01:01:16] ME. TURCOTTE: D'accord.

22   [01:01:17] LE TRIBUNAL: Okay ? On va -- je pense qu'on

23   va en avoir assez pour cette journée-là, okay ?

24   [01:01:20] ME. TURCOTTE: D'accord.

25   [01:01:21] LE TRIBUNAL: Procédons dans l'ordre. " --

71

1 débat sur le refus du demandeur de fournir les engagements

2 pour lesquels il n'y a pas eu d'objection - demande du -- de

3 la partie demanderesse en rejet sommaire du mémoire des

4 défenderesses ordonne aux parties défenderesses de produire

5 d'ici le 15 juin 2023 un tableau des objections à débattre et

6 une transcription de l'interrogatoire ; ordonne à la partie

7 demanderesse de produire d'ici le 15 juin 2023 sa demande

8 pour rejet sommaire -- sa demande pour rejet du mémoire des

9 parties défenderesses et une courte argumentation quand --

10 expliquant son refus de fournir les engagements requis à la

11 suite de son interrogatoire du 21 décembre 2022 pour lesquels

12 il n'y avait pas eu d'objections." Alors... voilà. Vous

13 allez noter aussi que... et là, ce sera plus dans les -- les

14 -- les -- les -- les -- les conclusions, Madame Étienne, mais

15 en dessous des conclusions. "Le tribunal souligne que tout

16 ce qui précède a été expliqué en anglais à la partie

17 demanderesse." Okay. Est-ce que --

18

19   [ANGLAIS]

20

21   [01:07:33] LE TRIBUNAL: Est-ce que j'ai des

22 disponibilités au tribunal des droits de la personne d'ici le

23 mois de juin, Madame Étienne ?

24   [01:07:38] GREFFIÈRE DE LA COUR: Je crois que j'ai pas

25 votre calendrier ici.

19

1   [01:07:40] LE TRIBUNAL: Vous avez -- avez-vous accès à

2 mon calendrier ?

3   [01:07:42] GREFFIÈRE DE LA COUR: Pas ici.

4   [01:07:43] LE TRIBUNAL: Oui, Maître Turcotte ? Vous

5 avez quelque chose à dire ?

6   [01:07:45] ME. TURCOTTE: Oui, on parlait du 19 avril

7 tantôt. Monsieur semblait avoir trouvé des disponibilités

8 dans son agenda.

9   [01:07:51] LE TRIBUNAL: Oui, sauf que --

10   [01:07:51] ME. TURCOTTE: Ça pourrait peut-être être une

11 bonne --

12   [01:07:53] LE TRIBUNAL: Oui, mais dans la mesure où

13 c'est moi qui -- qui vais l'entendre, il faut que je voie si

14 le 19 avril je suis disponible, mais je ne crois pas.

15   [01:08:00] ME. TURCOTTE: Je comprends.

16   [01:08:00] LE TRIBUNAL: Je vais... okay. Mais il va

17 falloir suspendre encore quelques instants. Je vais aller

18 vérifier mon calendrier pour les semaines qui viennent pour

19 voir quand est-ce --

20

21   [ANGLAIS]

22

23   [01:08:38] GREFFIÈRE DE LA COUR: Veuillez-vous lever --

24

25   [ANGLAIS]

1

2   [01:08:38] GREFFIÈRE DE LA COUR: -- demeurez à votre

3 place. L'audience du tribunal des droits de la personne est

4 suspendue.

5

6   (BRÈVE SUSPENSION DE SÉANCE)

7

8   [01:15:15] GREFFIÈRE DE LA COUR: Veuillez-vous lever.

9 L'audience du tribunal des droits de la personne se continue.

10 Veuillez-vous asseoir. Merci.

11

12   [ANGLAIS]

13

14   [01:15:41] LE TRIBUNAL: Alors, Madame Étienne, "Le

15 demandeur -- la partie demanderesse soulève qu'il croit que

16 la Juge soussignée ne peut rester saisie du dossier et

17 indique qu'il a l'intention de demander sa récusation. Il

18 dit avoir des motifs qu'il -- mais qu'il n'est pas prêt à les

19 donner aujourd'hui. À tout événement -- à tout événement, le

20 tribunal lui explique que la demande de récusation doit être

21 entendu par la Juge soussignée conformément à l'article 205

22 du code de procédure civile et qu'il doit évoquer les motifs

23 prévus à l'article 202. De plus, sa demande doit être faite

24 par écrit."

25

1   [ANGLAIS]

2

3   [01:17:37] LE TRIBUNAL: Madame Étienne, alors --

4

5   [ANGLAIS]

6

7   [01:17:44] LE TRIBUNAL: Alors, "Le tribunal explique

8   aussi que la demande devra être écrite -- " je pense que je

9   l'avais déjà dit peut-être. Alors, "Pour ces motifs le

10 tribunal ordonne à la partie demanderesse de produire sa --

11 une demande écrite justifiant ses motifs de récusations de la

12 Juge soussignée, appuyée d'une déclaration sous serment,

13 d'ici le 15 juin 2023."

14

15   [ANGLAIS]

16

17   [01:19:42] LE TRIBUNAL: Pas pour moi, Madame la Juge.

18

19   [ANGLAIS]

20

21   [01:20:21] LE TRIBUNAL: Bien. Alors, vous allez

22 recevoir --

23

24   [ANGLAIS]

25

Briaris Transcription Services

1   [01:20:29] LE TRIBUNAL: -- et d'ici --

2

3   [ANGLAIS]

4

5   [01:20:37] LE TRIBUNAL: Très bien.

6   [01:20:37] ME. TURCOTTE: Merci beaucoup, Madame la Juge.

7 Bonne journée.

8   [01:20:40] LE TRIBUNAL: Merci, Maître Turcotte.

9

10   [ANGLAIS]

11

12   ...FIN DE PROCÉDURE.

FRENCH LANGUAGE sERVICES
Inbox
Search for all messages with label Inbox
Remove label Inbox from this conversation

Court Interpretation - Ottawa <INTER-CITS@ontario.ca>   Mon,
                                                                  May 29,
                                                                  2:45 PM

to me

French

English

Translate message

Turn off for: French

Mr. Samuels,

The ministry pays for an interpreter's services on behalf of any party
to a Criminal, Civil, Family or Small Claims Court litigation who
requires French-language interpretation. The requesting party does
not need a CSD fee waiver in order to access such services, unlike
situations in which the language required is neither English nor
French. Please click on the hyperlinks below for the person
making the request to the ministry's website:
In English: https://www.ontario.ca/page/get-court-interpreter
En français : https://www.ontario.ca/fr/page/obtenir-les-services-
dun-interprete-judiciaire

Thank you,"

Victor Martens,
Coordonnateur des services d'interprétation   *Victor Martens*
                                                           Interpretation Services Co

Ministère du Procureur général
Palais de justice d'Ottawa
Services d'interprétation et de traduction judiciaires

161, rue Elgin, pièce 3240
Ottawa (Ontario) K2P 2K1

Téléphone : 613-239-1015
Courriel : INTER-CITS@ontario.ca

Vous êtes intéressé par l'interprétation judiciaire?
Cliquer afin d'apprendre comment
faire pour devenir interprète judiciaire indépendant.

AVIS DE CONFIDENTIALITÉ :

Le présent courriel est confidentiel et strictement
réservé à l'usage des destinataires. Si vous avez
reçu ce courriel par erreur, communiquez
immédiatement avec son auteur et détruisez
l'original et toute copie. Notez qu'il est strictement
interdit de divulguer, de reproduire ou de diffuser le
contenu de ce courriel. Tout nouvel envoi, toute
reproduction ou tout usage de ce courriel par une
personne autre que le destinataire prévu est
strictement interdit.
Merci.

Ministry of the Attorney Gen
Ottawa Courthouse
Court Interpretation and Tra

161 Elgin Street, room 3240
Ottawa, Ontario K2P 2K1

Telephone: 613-239-1015
Email: INTER-CITS@ontari

Interested in court interpreta
learn how to apply to becom

CONFIDENTIALITY NOTIC

The contents of this electror
confidential and strictly rese
intended recipients. If you re
please notify the sender imn
message as well as all copie
distribution or reliance on the
strictly prohibited.
Thank you.

Ontario ♔

Get a court interpreter

Learn how to get a court interpreter if you don't understand or speak the language of the court.

Overview

Court proceedings in Ontario take place in English or French. A court interpreter can help you understand what is being said in court when you don't speak the language of the court.

You have the right to a court interpreter if you need one.

The Ministry of the Attorney General provides court interpretation services in:

- any language required in criminal and child protection matters
- any language in civil, family and small claims court if the litigant qualifies for a fee waiver
- French in all civil, family and Small Claims Court matters
- sign language in all court matters
- any language when it is ordered by the court.

There are about 700 accredited freelance court interpreters that provide interpretation in:

- over 80 spoken languages
- American Sign Language
- Langue des signes du Québec

We provide more than 150,000 courtroom hours of interpretation every year.

MENU ›

Home > Canada's System of Justice > The Canadian Charter of Rights and Freedoms > Charterpedia

Section 14 – Right to an interpreter

← Previous   Table of contents   Next ↑

Provision

14. A party or witness in any proceedings who does not understand or speak the language in which the proceedings are conducted or who is deaf has the right to the assistance of an interpreter.

Similar provisions

Similar provisions may be found in the following Canadian laws and international instruments binding on Canada: section 2(g) of the *Canadian Bill of Rights*; section 15(1) of the *Official Languages Act*; and article 14(3)(f) of the *International Covenant on Civil and Political Rights*.

See also the following international, regional and comparative law instruments that are not legally binding on Canada but include similar provisions: article 6(3)(e) of the *European Convention for the Protection of Human Rights and Fundamental Freedoms*; and article 8(2)(a) of the *American Convention on Human Rights*.

In the criminal context, section 14 has a close relationship with section 7 (fundamental justice) and section 11(d) (fair trial) of the Charter (see the discussion further below). More generally, sections 15 (equality rights), 25 (aboriginal rights) and 27 (multicultural heritage) of the Charter also speak to the importance of the right to interpreter assistance. Section 27, which mandates that the Charter be interpreted in a manner consistent with the preservation and enhancement of the multicultural heritage of Canadians, is particularly relevant. In so far as a multicultural heritage is necessarily a multilingual one, it follows that a multicultural society can only be preserved and fostered if those who speak languages other than English and French are given real and substantive access to the criminal justice system (R. v. Tran, [1994] 2 S.C.R. 951).

Purpose

In the criminal context, the Supreme Court has referred to section 14 as serving three main purposes: i) to ensure that persons charged with an offence hear the case against them and have an opportunity to answer it; ii) as a right intimately related to our basic notions of justice, including the appearance of fairness; and iii) as a right intimately related to our society's claim to be multicultural, expressed in part through section 27 of the Charter. The Court also has referred to the underlying interests protected by section 14 as those of linguistic understanding and creating a level and fair playing field (Tran, supra, pages 977-978). As discussed below, however, the right also applies outside of the criminal context. While certain of the above-noted purposes of section 14 are particular to criminal proceedings, the other indicated purposes will likely be relevant outside of this context.

Analysis

1. General considerations

The right to the assistance of an interpreter is a fundamental right grounded in the rules of natural justice (Tran, supra, page 963; MacDonald v. City of Montreal, [1986] 1 S.C.R. 460 at page 499; Société des Acadiens v. Association of Parents, [1986] 1 S.C.R. 549 at page 621, per Wilson J., concurring).

82

It is not a separate language right, but, in the criminal context, it is a means of ensuring that criminal proceedings comply with the constitutional guarantee to a fair and public hearing found in section 11(d) of the Charter (*Tran, supra,* page 976). As such, section 14 should be understood in part by reference to sections 7 and 11 of the Charter, which protect a person's right to make full answer and defence, the right to have full disclosure of the case to be answered prior to making one's defence, and the right to a fair trial. Indeed, the close relationship of section 14 to these other Charter guarantees suggests that the right to interpreter assistance in the criminal context should be considered a "principle of fundamental justice" within the meaning of section 7 of the Charter (*Tran, supra,* page 976).

However, unlike many other sections of the Charter which apply in the criminal law context specifically, this section is more encompassing: it applies to "any proceedings". In *Tran,* the Supreme Court indicated that "the right under section 14 of the Charter is one held not only by accused persons, but also by parties in civil actions and administrative proceedings and by witnesses" (*Tran, supra,* page 995). However, the *Tran* decision also indicated that the discussion in that case applied to criminal proceedings and left open the possibility that other rules may apply to other proceedings (*Tran, supra,* page 961).

The principle of linguistic understanding which underpins the right to interpreter assistance should not be elevated to the point where those with difficulty communicating in or comprehending the language of the proceedings, be it English or French, are given or seen to be given unfair advantages over those who are fluent in the court's language (*Tran, supra,* page 978). Section 14 is concerned with linguistic understanding, but it is not intended to compensate for educational or cognitive deficiencies that may make it more difficult for an accused to understand and follow his or her own trial; this is an issue that the right to the assistance of counsel is intended to address (*Trottier c. R.,* 2018 QCCA 1693 at paras. 57-59 and 140).

(ii) Standard of interpretation

Section 14 of the Charter requires that the interpretation of the proceedings be continuous, precise, impartial, competent and contemporaneous. The standard that must be met in interpretation is not one of perfection, but is high (*Tran, supra,* page 985; *R. v. Rybak* (2008 ONCA 354, leave to appeal denied, [2008] S.C.C.A. No. 311). Appellate rulings suggest that an interpreter is presumed to have provided an accurate interpretation unless the claimant can demonstrate that the interpreter has not (*R. v. Titchener,* 2013 BCCA 64; *R. v. Match,* 2015 BCCA 271; see also *Nguyen v. R.,* 2013 QCCA 1127).

(a) Continuous

Breaks and interruptions in interpretation are not to be encouraged or allowed (*Tran, supra,* page 986).

(b) Precise

The interpretation must be, as close as can be, word-for-word and idea-for-idea; the interpreter must not "clean up" the evidence by giving it a form, a grammar or syntax that it does not have; the interpreter should make no commentary on the evidence; and the interpretation should be given only in the first person, *e.g.,* "I went to school" instead of "he says he went to school" (*Tran, supra,* pages 986-987). However, courts have acknowledged that interpretation requires certain "judgment calls"; not all words, phrases or concepts can be translated exactly to another language. As indicated previously, the standard is not that of perfection (*Match, supra,* paragraphs 8-9, 37).

(c) Impartial

Interpretation, particularly in a criminal context, should be objective and unbiased. Certain persons are disqualified, by reason of apprehension of bias, from acting as interpreter. Obviously a party litigant will not be permitted to interpret, but neither will a relative or friend of a party, the judge, nor a person closely connected to the events giving rise to a criminal charge. These rules may be relaxed if the proceedings are non-adversarial (*Tran, supra,* page 988). The practice of having an interpreter serve as both a witness and an interpreter is one which should be avoided in all but exceptional circumstances (*Tran, supra,* page 1002).

84

(d) Competent

An accused has a right to a competent interpreter and it is the judge's responsibility to ensure that the interpreter chosen possesses the necessary qualities (*Tran, supra,* pages 988-989). However, formal accreditation as an interpreter and competence are not the same thing: neither the presence nor absence of accreditation is dispositive of competence (*Rybak, supra,* paragraph 84). It has been considered, however, that accreditation provides a basis for a presumption of competence absent evidence to the contrary (*Titchener, supra,* at paragraph 23).

(e) Contemporaneous

It is generally preferable that interpretation be "consecutive" (after the words are spoken) rather than "simultaneous" (at the same time as words are spoken). However, the overriding consideration is that the interpretation be contemporaneous (*Tran, supra,* pages 989-990). Although consecutive translation is generally to be preferred, in the absence of any indicia that the interpretation was inadequate, there can be no violation of section 14 on account of the interpretation being simultaneous (*Nguyen, supra,* at paragraph 5; see also *R. v. Santhanarasa,* 2013 ONCA 779).

(iii) In the course of the proceedings

A claimant must establish that fault in respect of interpretation occurred in the course of the proceedings when a vital interest of the accused was involved — *i.e.,* while the case was being advanced — rather than at a stage which was extrinsic or collateral to the advancement of the case, such as an administrative or scheduling issue (*Tran, supra,* pages 991-994).

6. Remedy – Prejudice and reparation

It is crucial that, at the stage where it is being determined whether an accused's section 14 rights were in fact unjustifiably limited, courts not engage in speculation as to whether the lack of or lapse in interpretation in a specific instance made any difference to the outcome of the case, or as to whether the accused actually suffered prejudice (*Tran, supra*, pages 994 and 995). The prejudice is in being denied the right in the first place. The resulting prejudice actually suffered is a matter to be assessed in consideration of remedy under section 24(1) of the Charter (*Tran, supra*, page 995; *Mohammadian, supra* at paragraph 4).

While some case law at the lower court level has adopted a standard under which any errors must be "material" rather than "trivial", care must be taken not to thereby import a requirement of prejudice. "Material" in this context should be understood as an extension of the principle, also recognized in *Tran*, that the standard under section 14 is not one of perfection in interpretation: it is not an additional requirement to show prejudice arising out of non-trivial errors (see the discussion, *e.g.*, in *Mah, supra*, at paragraphs 21-26 and in *Bidgoli v. Canada (Minister of Citizenship and Immigration)*, 2015 FC 235 at paragraphs 10-16).

As a general rule, the appropriate remedy under section 24(1) of the Charter for a breach of section 14 will be the same as it would be under the common law and under statutory guarantees, such as section 650 of the *Criminal Code* or section 2(g) of the *Canadian Bill of Rights* — namely a re-hearing of the issue or proceeding in which the violation occurred (*Tran, supra*, page 1010). However, where appropriate, other remedies may be ordered, tailored to particular circumstances. For example, in one appellate case it was considered that prejudice that would have flowed from proceeding without an interpreter could have been addressed by adjourning proceedings to a date when an interpreter was available (*R. v. Pan*, 2012 ONCA 581 (Ont. C.A.); see also the comment in *Tran, supra*, pages 1010-1011, re remedying a violation in the course of the proceedings). Where an accused is able to demonstrate that he or she has suffered or will suffer prejudice over and above that which flows directly from the violation itself, such as having to incur the financial costs associated with a new trial, a court may find it appropriate to award an additional remedy under section 24(1), such as damages (*Tran, supra*, page 1010).

File No._____

IN THE SUPREME COURT OF CANADA

(ON APPEAL FROM AN INTERIM JUDGEMENT OF QUEBEC HUMAN RIGHTS TRIBUNAL AND THE SUPERIOR COURT OF QUEBEC)

BETWEEN:

RAYMOND CARBY-SAMUELS

APPLICANT (Appellant)

AND:

VILLE DE GATINEAU et al.

RESPONDENT (Respondent)

MEMORANDUM OF THE ARGUMENT OF THE APPLICANT (APPELLANT)

(Pursuant to Rule 25 of the Rules of the Supreme Court of Canada)

Raymond Carby-Samuels

Self-Represented Litigant,

Member, Canadian Bar Association

Tel: (514) 712-7516

Email: cosmopolita_rc@yahoo.com,

lawsociety.carby.samuels@utoronto.ca

Suite 325 - 207 Bank Street

Ottawa, Ontario K2P 2N2

DHC AVOCATS

Counsel for the Respondent

Suite 4500

800, Square Victoria

Montreal, Quebec H4Z 1J2

E-mail: mdaponte@dhcavocats.ca

TABLE OF CONTENTS

Page

PART I   OVERVIEW AND STATEMENT OF THE FACTS

A.   Overview

1.   This Court has recognized that the right to the assistance of an interpreter is a fundamental right grounded in the rules of natural justice (*Tran, supra*, page 963; *MacDonald v. City of Montreal*, [1986] 1 S.C.R. 460 at page 499; *Société des Acadiens v. Association of Parents*, [1986] 1 S.C.R. 549 at page 621, per Wilson J., concurring).

2.   In *Tran*, the Supreme Court indicated that "the right under section 14 of the Charter is one held not only by accused persons, but also by parties in civil actions and administrative proceedings and by witnesses" (*Tran, supra*, page 995).

3.   The particular issue in this case is whether courts and Tribunals in Quebec are required pursuant Supreme Court of Canada decisions, which are in turn based on the Canadian Charter of Rights and Freedoms to provide free access to court interpreter services to English-speaking individuals who are members of an Official Languages community;

4.   At present, and pursuant to Bill-96, unilingual English-speaking individuals who cannot afford to hire either a francophone lawyer or a private interpreter are being denied the ability to contest their rights in court proceedings, which enables French-only communications between the presiding judge and the opposing lawyer or self-represented litigants.

5.   Such a judicial milieu not only ignores Supreme Court of Canada decisions, which in turn are based upon the *Canadian Charter of Rights and Freedoms*, it also ignores social condition as a prohibited ground of discrimination pursuant to Section 10 of the *Quebec Charter of Rights*

and Freedoms because it limits the ability of English-speaking individuals who do not have the financial resources to either hire a francophone lawyer or a court interpreter:

> 10. Every person has a right to full and equal recognition and exercise of his human rights and freedoms, without distinction, exclusion or preference based on race, colour, sex, gender identity or expression, pregnancy, sexual orientation, civil status, age except as provided by law, religion, political convictions, language, ethnic or national origin, **social condition**, a handicap or the use of any means to palliate a handicap.
>
> **Discrimination exists where such a distinction, exclusion or preference has the effect of nullifying or impairing such right.**
>
> Section 14 - Interpreter (*Canadian Charter of Rights and Freedoms*)
>
> 14. A party or witness in any proceedings who does not understand or speak the language in which the proceedings are conducted or who is deaf has the right to the assistance of an interpreter.

6.   The Applicant, Raymond Samuels was conferred a decision by the Quebec Human Rights Commission to financially compensate him as a result of claims made against the Ville de Gatineau et al. regarding the activities of the Gatineau Police Services.

7.   The Quebec Human Rights Commission abandoned providing representation to the Applicant before the Quebec Human Rights Tribunal, which left the Applicant to his own to pursue a claim of financial compensation as a self-represented litigant.

8.   After having communicated entirely in English during the Quebec Human Rights Tribunal proceeding of December 21, 2023, the opposing law firm representing the Defendants began to refuse to communicate in English.

9.   On 15 March 2023, the Hon. Catherine Pilon, the presiding judge of the Quebec Human Rights Tribunal, and Mathieu Turcotte, the lawyer for the Defendants, communicated to each other exclusively in French, and that included discussions about the Applicant.

10.   Both Mathieu Turcotte and the presiding judge are bilingual.

11.   The Applicant stated their objections that their constitutional rights were being violated and respectfully demanded that the judge translate what they said and provide access to a free court interpreter in further court proceedings conducted in French.

12.   The presiding judge refused to translate the nature of what they were communicating to each other and denied access to any free court interpreter.

13.   The presiding judge stated that the Applicant would be responsible for hiring their own private court interpreter and that it was not the responsibility of the Quebec Human Rights Tribunal to provide such an interpreter. The judge continued to talk only in French to the opposing lawyer in a manner which prevented the Applicant from seeking to raise objections to any decisions they agreed to undertake.

14.   The presiding judge rendered an interim decision that it was the Applicant's responsibility to hire their own court interpreter and that the Tribunal bears no such responsibility to provide free access to court interpreter services as a natural right in a bilingual country.

15.   The Applicant sought to make a Leave to Appeal to the Superior Court of Quebec as part of an effort to transfer their file from the Quebec Human Rights Tribunal to the Superior Court of Quebec as a result of the Applicant's experience of discrimination perpetrated by the Tribunal for not having the social condition to be able to hire their own private interpreter. However, the opposing bilingual law firm once again refused to communicate in English with the Superior Court of Quebec, correspondingly refusing to provide free access to court interpreter services that would be the right of the Applicant if they were French-speaking in Ontario.

16   The representative of the opposing law firm and the Quebec Superior Court asserted Bill-96 as the "common language of Quebec," which enabled denying access to justice to non-francophones who are not able to afford to hire a francophone lawyer or private interpreter.

17.   The Quebec Superior Court judge further elaborated in their interim written decision that they had no authority to provide free access to a court interpreter in spite of the fact that Ontario courts have declared through a Government of Ontario website that they provide "more than 150,000 hours every year" in free court interpretation services. Such statistical representation points to the magnitude of the complete denial of such services to non-francophones in Quebec, which fundamentally includes English-speaking language communities.

18.   Lower court rulings effectively weaponize the French language against people who cannot speak French, who are as a result denied the ability to apply to a court of competent jurisdiction in Quebec if they cannot understand French during a Quebec court or tribunal hearing, lack financial resources to hire a private interpreter, and the court or tribunal refuses to provide court interpreter services.

19.   The Applicant submits that the subject matter at issue is of such profound constitutional importance, affecting such a large segment of the population of the Province of Quebec, (and the population of Canada that seeks to apply to a court or tribunal for judicial review as a result of personal or business activities in that province) that it is an issue deserving of consideration and final disposition by the Supreme Court of Canada.

B. Background to the Current Dispute

20.   The Quebec Human Rights Commission, after having investigated human rights complaints against officers of the Gatineau Police Services, assessed $60,000 in damages and pursued a formal claim to the Quebec Human Rights Tribunal.

21.   DHC Avocats, which is representative of the Defendants, had communicated to the plaintiff entirely in English during a Quebec Human Rights Tribunal hearing on December 21, 2022. However, in a subsequent Quebec Human Rights Tribunal hearing on March 15, 2023, this same law firm began to communicate entirely in French.

22.   The plaintiff objected to the presiding Judge Catherine Pilon's tribunal court hearing banter entirely in French with the representative of DHC Avocats, which included discussions regarding the plaintiff that the plaintiff could not participate in because he couldn't understand their communications with each other in French.

23.   Judge Catherine Pilon replied in English that the plaintiff would need to hire and pay for his own private interpreter and then continued legal banter with DHC Avocats entirely in French, fully well knowing that the plaintiff couldn't understand what was being said despite the plaintiff's constitutional objections.

24.   In the face of such violations of rights pursuant to Section 14 of the *Canadian Charter of Rights and Freedoms*, the plaintiff pursued both an appeal and transfer of his file to the Quebec Superior Court. However, during the May 24, 2023 hearing, the plaintiff was further denied a free court interpreter in the face of the calculated efforts of DHC Avocats to wilfully refrain from speaking in English in order to exploit the plaintiff's lack of French comprehension.

25.   The Quebec Court of Appeal indicated in written correspondence that the plaintiff would also be denied access to an interpreter regarding any appeal launched through their system.

C.   Judicial History

26.   The Applicant's efforts to pursue a claim in the Quebec court system against the City of Gatineau which had been originally endorsed by the Quebec Human Rights Commission before he became a self-represented litigant have been stalled because the Applicant cannot understand the French which is being used in hearings pursuant to communications between the judges and opposing lawyers.

PART II   STATEMENT OF THE ISSUES

27.   The primary question at issue in the present appeal is whether a court hearing conducted partially or wholly in French in which a court or human rights tribunal in Quebec doesn't provide interpreter services to a member of the English-speaking Official Language group, consistent with efforts by courts outside of Quebec to provide access to interpreter services to francophones, as a direct response to previous Supreme Court of Canada rulings, is constitutionally offensive to the spirit and integrity of Canada as a bilingual country that consists of English and French Official Languages groups.

28.   The Applicant contends that as a member of the English-speaking Official Language group, he is entitled to the same range of court interpreter services made available to francophones (and other language minorities) outside of the Province of Quebec.

29.   Courts and Tribunals outside of Quebec have sought to provide court interpreter services without charge to francophones as a direct result of constitutional obligations imposed by previous Supreme Court of Canada decisions. Quebec courts and tribunals in our constitutional system of governance are under the same obligations to provide such court interpreter services, which the Supreme Court of Canada has deemed to be a "natural right."

30.   The judges presiding over the Quebec Human Rights Tribunal and the Superior Court hearings were obliged to immediately stop the hearing as soon as the Applicant communicated that he could not understand what was being said. However, this was not done by either judge, who continued the hearings with banter which the Applicant couldn't challenge because he could not understand what was being said between the judge and opposing lawyer.

31.   The judges presiding over the Quebec Human Rights Tribunal and the Superior Court hearings did not provide the Applicant with any time to get the support of a private court interpreter service even if he was willing to do so, and as a result, the proceedings should be nullified, including any decision which was made by the Court that was associated with a hearing in which the Applicant didn't have access to interpreter services;

32.   The Quebec Human Rights Tribunal providing ensuing judgement in French only, when the presiding judge is completely bilingual, further underscores disrespect to the Applicant as a member of an Official Languages group.

33.   The case raises issues of public and national importance along with questions of law arising henceforth:

(a)   Does a court, or specifically a human rights tribunal hearing conducted partially or wholly in French, with no interpreter services provided by the court to a litigant who cannot understand what is being said in banter between the judge or the opposing lawyer during the hearing constitute a violation of the fundamental language rights of an English-speaking member of an Official Language group who seeks to avail their human and other civil rights in a Quebec courtroom?

(b)   Does the affirmation of the integrity of *the Canadian Charter of Rights and Freedoms* fundamentally require that courts and tribunals ensure that all Canadians understand the language that is being used in proceedings, as affirmed in previous Supreme Court of Canada decisions?

(c)   Does Canada's status as an officially bilingual country as affirmed in the *Canadian Charter of Rights and Freedoms* oblige all courts and tribunals across

Canada to ensure that all members of these Official Languages group are provided

with free court interpreter services to ensure that each respective Official

Languages group will not be linguistically impaired in any court or tribunal

hearing?

(d)   Are judges required to provide judgement in the preferred language expressed by

the member of an Official Languages group?

(e)   Are Quebec courts required to respect decisions of the Supreme Court of Canada

that are designed to promote access to justice by members of Official Languages

groups along with the rights of language minorities, including Indigenous groups,

pursuant to multicultural provision of the *Canadian Charter of Rights and*

Freedoms?

(f)   Does the failure of a Canadian court or tribunal to provide universal access to

language interpretation services to both Official Language groups, regardless of

where they seek to apply to a court of competent jurisdiction to avail their rights,

create an unconstitutional systemic barrier regarding basic access to justice,

which amounts to extinguishing guaranteed rights and freedoms?

(g)   Can the French language be advanced by extinguishing the rights of non-

francophones who don't have the financial means to either hire a francophone

lawyer or pay for private court interpreter services?

(h)   Did the refusal to provide the Applicant with full and contemporaneous

translation of the banter between the Quebec Human Rights Tribunal's judge and

the opposing lawyer deny the right of the Applicant to be present during the whole judicial proceeding and his right to make a full answer and defence to any representations asserted by the Defendants' lawyer?

(i)   Did the refusal to provide the Applicant with full and contemporaneous translation of the banter between the Superior Court of Quebec's judge and the opposing lawyer deny the right of the Applicant to be present during the whole judicial proceeding and his right to make a full answer and defence to any representations asserted the Defendants' lawyer?

Historical and Constitutional Analysis

34.   The architects of *the Canadian Charter of Rights and Freedoms,* through Sections 15(1) and 24(1), sought to facilitate a context for Canadians to apply to a court of competent jurisdiction in order to challenge any deemed infringements to equality before the law based upon the principle that Canada is a bilingual country that also respects everyone's multicultural heritage as affirmed in Section 27.

35.   It is inconceivable that the architects of the *Canadian Charter of Rights and Freedoms* would have intended that any Canadian would be denied the ability to obtain relief from the court as a result of a claim regarding breaches of equality rights perpetrated by the police or another government agency as a result a failure by the court to ensure access to interpreter services asserted by the Supreme Court of Canada as a "natural right."

36.   If the Supreme Court of Canada does not seek to assert the constitutional requirement that Quebec courts have to ensure language is not a barrier to anyone who seeks to apply to a court or tribunal of competent jurisdiction regarding infringements to equality and other rights guaranteed by the *Canadian Charter of Rights and Freedoms,* then it cannot be said that Canadians who are

not francophones have rights in a Quebec court hearing environment in which language is

axiomatic to the ability of opposing litigants to proceed with a trial.

PART III   GROUNDS FOR LEAVE TO APPEAL

37.   The Quebec Court of Appeal erred in law by not having an established policy to enable litigants of the English Official Language group (and other language minorities pursuant to the Canadian Multiculturalism Act) to have access to free court interpreter services.

38.   The Superior Court of Quebec erred in law by failing to recognize the right of the Applicant to have access to free court interpreter services to affirm the Applicant's right to be present throughout its court hearing process.

39.   The Quebec Human Rights Tribunal erred in law by failing to recognize the right of the Applicant to have access to free court interpreter services to affirm the Applicant's right to be present throughout its hearing; it erred in law by making a written judgement only in French after the Applicant declared English to be his preferred Official Language of court correspondence.

PART IV   COSTS

39.   The Applicant requests that he be granted costs of this Application in any event of the cause.

PART V   ORDER SOUGHT

40.   The Applicant respectfully requests an Order granting Leave to Appeal from an interim judgement of the Superior Court and an interim judgement of the Quebec Human Rights Tribunal (reinforced in an emailed affirmation by the Quebec Court of Appeal as a policy of the

Court of Appeal) dated May 23, 2023, which refused to recognize the right of the Applicant to be

provided with free court interpreter services.

ALL OF WHICH IS RESPECTFULLY SUBMITTED this 10th day of July, 2023

        Raymond Samuels

        Member, Canadian Bar Association

        Self-represented litigant

        Per: _____

PART VI   AUTHORITIES

www.ingramcontent.com/pod-product-compliance
Lightning Source LLC
Chambersburg PA
CBHW081821200326
41597CB00023B/4342